WATCHMAN ON THE WALLS

Understanding Israel's Modern Struggle

ALFREDO M. LIM

In memory of my spiritual father

Arthur Katz

(13 February 1929–28 June 2007)

Your prophetic voice and unwavering commitment to truth opened my eyes to the mystery of Israel. Your life and message stirred something eternal in me. This work would not exist without the seeds you've sown in my heart.

CONTENTS

ACKNOWLEDGEMENTS

To my beloved wife, Josefine—thank you for loving and supporting me through every season. You believed in me when I couldn't, stayed with me through the long nights and early mornings, lifted me in your prayers. I've watched you give so much of your time and heart to editing this book. Every page carries a piece of your love and sacrifice, and I will always be grateful to God for you.

To Joanna, our first-born—you were with me every step of the way in making this book a reality. From the earliest concepts to the final design, you carried the weight of the work with excellence and love. Thank you for your heart, your creativity, and the joy you bring to everything you touch.

To our second daughter, Janelle—your kind heart and gentle strength have been a constant blessing to me. You've stood with me with encouragement and care, always finding thoughtful ways to lift my spirits and the joy your children bring fills my heart with gratitude.

To our youngest, Janica, and her husband, Matt—I can't thank you enough for the love and support you've given me. You've supported me and your mum in every season, encouraged us when we needed it most, and cared for our family with such generosity of heart. Knowing you are always there has been one of the greatest blessings of my life, and I am forever grateful for you both.

To my mentor, Terry Edwards—during my foundational years as a Christian, you faithfully poured into my life. Your guidance, training, and belief in me shaped not only this book but my journey as a leader. Though you are no longer with us, your influence remains a lasting part of my calling.

And to my dear friend, Anne Hamilton—your encouragement for me to write and your example as an author gave me the inspiration I needed to take this path. I am deeply thankful for your influence and support.

And to all who have stood with me, prayed for me, and encouraged me along the way—this book is as much yours as it is mine.

Above all, I offer my deepest gratitude to God, Who has been my strength, guide, and constant source of inspiration. Without His grace, this book would never have been possible. This book is ultimately His story written through me.

"For this reason I kneel before the Father, from Whom every family in heaven and on earth derives its name. I pray that out of His glorious riches He may strengthen you with power through His Spirit in your inner being, so that Christ may dwell in your hearts through faith. And I pray

that you, being rooted and established in love, may have power, together with all the Lord's holy people, to grasp how wide and long and high and deep is the love of Christ, and to know this love that surpasses knowledge—that you may be filled to the measure of all the fullness of God.

Now to Him Who is able to do immeasurably more than all we ask or imagine, according to His power that is at work within us, to Him be glory in the church and in Christ Jesus throughout all generations, for ever and ever! Amen."

Ephesians 3:14–21

PREFACE

Answering the Call:
Why I Wrote This Book

"I have posted watchmen on your walls, Jerusalem; they will never be silent day or night. You who call on the Lord, give yourselves no rest, and give Him no rest till He establishes Jerusalem and makes her the praise of the earth."

Isaiah 62:6–7

This book was born out of holy unrest.

For years, I lived as a believer in Jesus with sincere devotion to the Church and the Great Commission. I taught the Word, prayed for revival, and served the Body of Christ with joy. And yet, there was a stirring deep within—an ache I could not name. Something was missing. Something central.

That ache led me to ask a dangerous question: *What about Israel?*

It wasn't a question I came to easily. Like many Christians, I had been taught to see the Old Testament as history and the New Testament as fulfillment. Israel was, at best, a backdrop to the gospel. At worst, she was a failed nation that had forfeited her role in God's plan.

And that question began to be answered the day I met Art Katz. And as I sat under his piercing prophetic voice—everything began to shift. His voice was not the voice of a man seeking influence. Art's words did not entertain—they interrogated. He wasn't trendy. He wasn't easy to listen to. But he was true. Every time I heard him speak, it felt as if the Spirit of God was drilling through my comfortable assumptions and calling me to something deeper, harder, and infinitely more real.

Art talked about Israel in a way I had never heard before. Not through the lens of politics or end-times speculation, but with prophetic gravity. He spoke of God's covenant with a people whom He would not abandon, and of a Church that had grown forgetful of its own roots. He often said to me,

> *"The Church's treatment of Israel is the litmus test of its understanding of God."*

That was a turning point for me.

It was as if a veil began to lift. Suddenly, the prophets weren't distant figures of ancient history—they were burning voices calling out to a wayward generation. I started to see the Scriptures as a unified testimony of a God who keeps covenant even when His people fail. I began to understand that to grasp God's heart, one must wrestle with His dealings with Israel—both the glory and the judgment.

I saw that Israel was not a theological side note. She was central to the story of redemption. I began to understand that God's covenant with Abraham had not been annulled. His promises had not expired. The people of Israel, the land of Israel, and the city of Jerusalem were not simply ancient themes—they were present realities and future prophecies.

And suddenly, I could no longer remain silent.

This book is my attempt to share that awakening—to extend the same call that wrecked me for complacent Christianity and pressed me into a deeper, more prophetic walk with God. It is written not as an academic textbook, nor as a political manifesto, but as a trumpet blast. It is for those who sense that something profound is unfolding in our world today, and who want to understand how Israel fits into that picture.

To the One Who Feels the Stirring...

This book is for the pastor who senses there's more to the biblical story.

For the intercessor who has felt the Spirit's groaning for Jerusalem.

For the believer who cannot ignore the headlines, but longs to hear the Spirit's voice above the noise.

For those who feel the call—but haven't yet found the language.

If that's you, I pray that these pages will serve as both compass and commission. May they draw you deeper into the Scriptures, higher in your worship, and further into God's purposes for Israel and the nations.

You are invited into a sacred calling—to stand on the wall, to see through God's eyes, and to join the story of Israel's redemption.

May this book ignite a fire in your heart. May it cause you to take your place as a watchman on the wall. And may it press you closer to the Cross—where all true revelation begins.

This book was written so that those who hear the Spirit's voice calling them as a watchman would say, "Yes, Lord. I will watch. I will weep. I will not be silent."

We are living in prophetic days. The winds are shifting. The walls are trembling. Now is not the time for silence.

Now is the time for watchmen to arise.

May you find your place on the wall.

INTRODUCTION

Watchman on the Walls: Understanding Israel's Modern Struggle is a timely and powerful exploration of the nation of Israel through a prophetic, theological, and current-events lens. As war rages, alliances shift, and Jerusalem becomes the focus of global tension, this book equips believers to understand the spiritual significance of Israel's modern challenges.

Rooted in Scripture and rich in historical insight, this book calls the Church to take its rightful place as watchmen—alert, prayerful, and discerning. With clarity and compassion, it addresses Israel's past, analyses the present crisis, and looks ahead to what the prophets foresaw.

Whether you are a pastor, intercessor, student of prophecy, or simply a Christian wanting to understand how Israel fits into God's plan, *Watchman on the Walls* is your guide to engaging with Israel's story from a place of truth, faith, and hope.

A Nation, A Crisis, A Calling

Israel. A tiny nation no larger than some counties in the world—yet it constantly occupies global headlines, stirs spiritual warfare, and sits at the centre of both history and destiny. Why? What is it about Israel that commands such attention, inspires such controversy, and evokes such passion—especially among believers?

In recent years, Israel has once again become a flashpoint. War has erupted in its cities and border regions. Political turmoil has shaken its internal unity. Media battles and international criticism swirl around it. For many, this is simply another chapter in a long, troubled history. But for those who understand Scripture, it's much more.

So why does Israel matter? And why now, in these troubled times, is the Spirit of God stirring His people to turn their attention to Jerusalem?

This book is a result of these questions and the stirring of a watchman's burden. As believers, we are not called to be passive spectators of the headlines. We are called to understand the times, discern God's hand, and pray with insight and urgency. We are called to the walls—not with weapons, but with wisdom, worship, and unwavering faith.

What This Book Is—And Isn't

This book is not a partisan defence of modern Israel's politics. It is not a speculative end-times chart. It is not driven by fear or sentiment.

It is a call to clarity.

A return to Scripture.

A summons to the wall.

Each chapter is built to equip you—with prophetic understanding, biblical foundations, and practical guidance for how to live as a watchman in these times. We will explore the covenantal heartbeat of God, the mystery of Jew-Gentile unity, the spiritual war surrounding Jerusalem, and the Church's responsibility in this unfolding hour.

You will find teaching, yes—but also exhortation. You will be challenged to pray differently, think differently, and perhaps even weep differently.

The question is no longer optional. "Why Israel? Why now?" is a question the Church must answer—or risk missing one of the most vital aspects of God's end-time purposes.

A Word to the Church

We are living in times of shaking. Nations are in uproar. And as mentioned before, Israel finds herself at the centre of global attention and conflict. This is not a coincidence. It is divine orchestration.

The Church is at a crossroads. We are facing increasing cultural hostility, doctrinal confusion, and global upheaval. Yet in the midst of all this, God is drawing our attention to Israel again—not as a distraction, but as a revelation.

Why?

Because how we view Israel reveals how we view God. If He is faithful to His covenant with them, then He will be faithful to His promises to us. If His dealings with Israel are ongoing, then our theology must make room for mystery, mercy, and the unfolding drama of redemption. If we ignore Israel, we risk misunderstanding the very character of the God we worship.

This is not merely about theology. It is about identity. The Church cannot understand her place without understanding Israel's. **We are not a replacement—we are the grafted-in.** And if we are to be ready for the return of Jesus, we must learn to watch, pray, and partner with God's heart for His firstborn nation.

This is not merely a study guide or historical review. It is a call to action, a prophetic trumpet, and a discipleship tool. It will lead you to Scripture, but also to the altar. It will challenge you to think differently, pray differently, and live differently. It's my prayer that these pages lead you into deeper understanding and renewed love for God.

As you read, you may notice that some Scriptures and thoughts appear more than once. This is intentional. Certain truths have a way of speaking to us again and again, each time with fresh meaning and depth. My desire is that these repeated verses will not feel redundant, but like familiar friends—returning to remind, reassure, and draw you closer to the heart of God.

PART 1

THE WATCHMAN'S CALL

CHAPTER 1

The Church's Prophetic Calling — Watchmen on The Walls

"Son of man, I have made you a watchman for the people of Israel; so hear the word I speak and give them warning from Me."

Ezekiel 33:7

The Church's Role Beyond a Nation or Land

The struggle of Israel is not merely geopolitical or ethnic—it is a spiritual battle that involves the whole Body of Christ. The Church is called into a prophetic role, charged with vigilance and intercession in these critical times.

Called to Watch

Ezekiel's appointment as a watchman[1] is a vivid Old Testament example of God's call to vigilance. Positioned high on the city walls, a watchman's task was to be alert and to warn the people of approaching danger.

This responsibility carries into the New Testament Church. We are to discern spiritual movements, watch over God's people, and pray without ceasing.

"Therefore keep watch, because you do not know on what day your Lord will come."

Matthew 24:42

This is an active, costly calling, not passive observation. The watchman stands in the gap—a spiritual sentinel burdened for Israel and the nations.

A Burden That Wakes the Sleeper

Many believers are unaware or disengaged from Israel's prophetic significance, but the watchman cannot be indifferent or asleep.

This burden produces sorrow for the spiritual state of the people and compels urgent prayer and action. The coming days will reveal who stands and who falls, underscoring the urgency of the watchman's role.

Intercession: More Than Prayer

Intercession is the heart of watchmanship—not merely petition but spiritual warfare. Biblical examples show how God moves in response to intercession:

- Moses interceded for Israel when they sinned with the golden calf (Exodus 32:11–14).

- Daniel's fervent prayer helped bring God's restoration to Israel's captivity (Daniel 9).

- Nehemiah's prayers opened the way for the rebuilding of Jerusalem's walls (Nehemiah 1).

Israel remains a battlefield for spiritual authority today, and the Church must pray with wisdom, urgency, and faith.

Living as Watchmen

To live as a watchman demands holiness, spiritual discernment, and courage. It requires embracing daily the suffering and sacrifice of following Christ's example.

The Church must not be caught off guard but be ready to stand firm in faith and truth no matter the cost.

"Watch and pray so that you will not fall into temptation. The spirit is willing, but the flesh is weak."

Matthew 26:41

The Reward and Responsibility

Watchmen carry grave responsibility. Failure to warn the people results in judgment. Faithful watchmen participate in God's redemptive glory and salvation of many.

> *"But if the watchman sees the sword coming and does not blow the trumpet to warn the people and the sword comes and takes someone's life, that person's life will be taken because of their sin, but I will hold the watchman accountable for their blood."*

Ezekiel 33:6

The prophetic calling is foundational—it is the heartbeat of a Church awake to God's eternal plan.

CHAPTER 2

The Watchman's Mandate

Theme:

*The Calling and Responsibility of Believers
to Be Spiritual Watchmen over Israel,
the Church, and the Times*

The Sleepless Wall

On the ancient walls of Jerusalem, the footsteps of watchmen echo through the centuries. Today, security guards patrol with high-tech gear, but the principle remains unchanged: **stay awake, stay alert, protect what matters.**

In the spiritual realm, God is raising up a new kind of watchman—those who will not sleep through the unfolding drama of God's purposes on the earth.

These watchmen are not necessarily pastors or prophets. They are believers with eyes open to heaven's agenda and ears tuned to God's voice. They see the danger before it hits, sense the spiritual atmosphere behind the headlines, and refuse to remain passive.

1. Who Is a Watchman?

Biblically, a watchman held a high place of visibility and responsibility. From their vantage point, they could see danger coming from afar and sound the alarm.

Spiritually, God calls His people to this role in every generation. A **watchman** is someone who:

- ✡ **Discerns** the times through spiritual eyes
- ✡ **Intercedes** with urgency and insight
- ✡ **Speaks** truth, even when unpopular
- ✡ **Warns** and awakens others
- ✡ **Remains faithful** when others fall asleep

2. Watchmen Over Israel

The calling to be a watchman is inseparable from God's covenant with **Israel**. Isaiah is clear:

> *"You who call on the Lord, give yourselves no rest, and give Him no rest till He establishes Jerusalem and makes her the praise of the earth."*

Isaiah 62:6b–7

This is not poetic language—it is a **divine command**.

To watch over Israel means:

- ✡ **Praying** for her peace (Psalm 122:6)

- ✡ **Standing** against spiritual and physical attacks

- ✡ **Blessing** Israel, not politically, but prophetically

- ✡ **Interceding** for the veil to be lifted and salvation to come (Romans 10:1)

To ignore Israel's pain, or remain silent in her distress, is to **fail the wall.**

3. Watchmen Over the Church

The Church is also in urgent need of watchmen. Many within the Body of Christ have grown:

- ✡ Spiritually dull

- ✡ Doctrinally compromised

- ✡ Comfortable and unprepared for the hour at hand

The watchman's trumpet must now **sound an alarm:**

"Blow the trumpet in Zion; sound the alarm on My holy hill."

Joel 2:1a

Watchmen in the Church must:

- ✡ **Guard doctrine** against deception

- ✡ **Call to repentance** in love

- ✡ **Awaken apathy** through truth

- ✡ **Prepare the Bride** for the coming King

This is not a role of superiority, but of servanthood and sacrifice. Many prophets were **mocked, rejected, or killed—** yet they were faithful to the mandate.

4. Watchmen Over the Times

We are living in **prophetic days.** The convergence of signs is no coincidence. Watchmen must:

- Be like the **sons of Issachar,** who understood the times (1 Chronicles 12:32)

- **Interpret** events not by media, but by **Scripture**

- Speak with clarity and conviction—not driven by fear or political trends, but by **the Word and the Spirit**

The call is not just to watch the news but to **watch with spiritual intelligence.** It is not about speculation or date-setting—but discernment.

5. The Cost and the Reward

To be a watchman is costly:

- You carry **spiritual burdens** that are not your own

- You often feel **alone** in your urgency

- You may be **misunderstood,** even by fellow believers

But the reward is greater:

- **Intimacy with God** in intercession

- **Authority in prayer**

- **Insight into the prophetic calendar**

✡ **Participation** in God's redemptive work in Israel and the nations

"And the Lord said, 'Who then is that faithful and wise steward, whom his master will make ruler over his household, to give them their portion of food in due season? Blessed is that servant whom his master will find so doing when he comes.'"

Luke 12:42–43 NKJV

The Wall Needs Watchers

The walls are shaking. The signs are here. Israel is in crisis. The Church is asleep in many places. This is not the hour for silence, apathy, or distraction. This is the hour for **watchmen to rise.**

Ask yourself:

✡ Am I willing to say "yes" to the call, even if it costs me?

✡ Am I cultivating a lifestyle of **watchfulness and prayer?**

✡ Am I willing to speak when others remain silent?

Let heaven hear your voice. Let Israel feel your intercession. Let the Church be awakened by your trumpet.

Will you take your place?

"I will stand my watch and set myself on the rampart, and watch to see what He will say to me, and what I will answer when I am corrected."

Habakkuk 2:1 NKJV

Scriptures for Further Study:

✡ Psalm 122:6–7 NKJV — *"Pray for the peace of Jerusalem: 'May they prosper who love you. Peace be within your walls, Prosperity within your palaces.'"*

✡ Romans 10:1 NKJV — *"Brethren, my heart's desire and prayer to God for Israel is that they may be saved."*

✡ Acts 20:28 — *"Keep watch over yourselves and all the flock of which the Holy Spirit has made you overseers. Be shepherds of the church of God, which He bought with His own blood."*

✡ Revelation 3:2 — *"Wake up! Strengthen what remains and is about to die, for I have found your deeds unfinished in the sight of My God."*

✡ Luke 12:37 NKJV — *"Blessed are those servants whom the master, when he comes, will find watching. Assuredly, I say to you that he will gird himself and have them sit down to eat, and will come and serve them."*

PART 2

GOD'S COVENANT AND ISRAEL'S IDENTITY

CHAPTER 3

The God of Israel — Covenant, Calling, and Controversy

"The issue of Israel is the issue of God, and it's an issue that is not finished yet."

—Art Katz, *The Church and the Jew*

The Olive Tree in the Storm

The wind swept over the Judean hills, where time and nature had carved their testimony into every stone and tree. Just outside Hebron stood an old olive tree, weather-beaten and twisted, yet somehow still bursting with life. Its trunk, split and scarred by centuries of exposure, bore scars like battle wounds. Fires had licked its bark. Storms had lashed its branches. Yet, against all odds—it stood.

That tree, in its quiet defiance against the elements, was a living parable. It embodied the resilience of Israel: wounded, misunderstood, maligned—and yet miraculously preserved. Not by chance. Not by mere nationalism. But by *covenant.*

The story of Israel cannot be rightly told by newspapers or political analysts. It is the story of a people chosen by God—not because they earned it, but because He had a purpose. Israel is not just a nation; she is a testimony. Her survival in the face of annihilation is not just history—it's prophecy unfolding. Like the olive tree, Israel remains rooted in the soil of divine promise, and though history has tried to shake her, she stands—because God has said she will.

The Ancient Covenant: A Divine Initiative

Before there was a people, a Torah, a land, or even a city named Jerusalem—there was a covenant. God's covenant with Abraham in Genesis 12 was not the result of Abraham's virtue or vision. It was born from the sovereign initiative of God. He called a man out of pagan obscurity to begin a lineage that would carry His name, His purposes, and His glory to the ends of the earth.

This was not a contract between equals. It was not dependent on human performance. It was a *unilateral, eternal* declaration:

> *"The Lord had said to Abram ... 'I will make you into a great nation, and I will bless you ... and all peoples on earth will be blessed through you.'"*

Genesis 12:1–3

It was God binding Himself to a people for the sake of His name and the redemption of the world.

Covenant vs. Contract

In our modern thinking, we often confuse God's covenant with human contracts—agreements that can be revised, renegotiated, or annulled. But the covenant with Israel is not a temporary legal arrangement; it is an *eternal commitment.*

"So you will be My people, and I will be your God."

Jeremiah 30:22

This is why Replacement Theology[2] is more than a doctrinal error—it is a misrepresentation of God's nature. If God can abandon His covenant with Israel, how can the Church trust His covenant with them?

Paul, anticipating this very distortion, wrote forcefully in Romans 11:

"I ask then: Did God reject His people? By no means! I am an Israelite myself, a descendant of Abraham, from the tribe of Benjamin."

Romans 11:1

"For God's gifts and His call are irrevocable."

Romans 11:29

The Church is not a *replacement* of Israel; it is the *grafted-in partner.*[3] To miss this is to distort not just Israel's place—but the nature of the gospel itself.

The Covenant Still Stands

The modern Church, even in its good intentions, has often inherited a theology that downplays Israel's role. Some do it theologically, others practically—through silence. But either way, the result is the same: **Israel is treated as irrelevant** to the New Testament Church. That is not only poor theology—it is dangerous.

This is why Israel is not a side issue—it is central to how we understand God's justice, faithfulness, and mercy.

The Scandal of Divine Election

Let's face it: God's choice of Israel is offensive. Why would God elect a people known more for their failures than their faith? Why would He stake His reputation on a nation that has historically resisted Him?

Because God is not afraid of scandal. He delights in choosing the weak and the foolish to shame the strong. His election of Israel isn't about Israel's righteousness—it's about *His own name*.

> *"It was not because you were more in number than any other people that the* Lord *set His love on you and chose you, for you were the fewest of all peoples, but it is because the* Lord *loves you and is keeping the oath that He swore to your fathers."*

> Deuteronomy 7:7–8a ESV

Israel becomes the mirror of divine mercy—proving that God does not abandon covenant, even when His people do.

Israel in the Furnace

The prophetic scriptures make it clear: the regathering of Israel would not be the end of her journey, but the beginning of a deeper refining.

> *"...I will refine them like silver and test them like gold. They will call on My name and I will answer them; I will say, 'They are My people' and they will say, 'The Lord is our God.'"*

Zechariah 13:9

Modern Israel is largely secular. She is often torn by internal division and surrounded by external threats. But this is not a contradiction of prophecy—it is the *fulfilment* of it. The restoration is both physical and spiritual. The physical return to the land precedes the *spiritual return to God.*

Art Katz often referred to this as the **furnace of affliction**—a divine fire that purges the dross and prepares a remnant for the coming of the Lord.

A Controversy Among the Nations

Why does the world rage over one tiny sliver of land?

Because Jerusalem is not just real estate. It is the **throne site of God**, the place from which Messiah will rule. The controversy over Israel is not geopolitical—it is *spiritual.* There is a cosmic contention over the purposes of God in the earth, and Israel is at the epicentre.[4]

I can still remember Art telling me, *"If you want to know where we are on God's calendar, look at Jerusalem."* Every war, every UN resolution, every missile is a footnote to a greater reality: **God is preparing the earth for His Kingdom.**

Why the Land Matters

Many believers wonder why land matters. Isn't it all spiritual now?

Not to God.

From Genesis onward, the land is part of the promise. It's not a side note. God gave Abraham not only a people—but a place. The land of Israel is not symbolic; it is *sacred territory,* chosen by God for His dwelling.

> *"For the Lord has chosen Zion, He has desired it for His dwelling, saying, 'This is My resting place forever and ever; here I will sit enthroned, for I have desired it.'"*

Psalm 132:13

That's why the battles over land and borders are not merely political—they are prophetic. The land remains contested because the enemy knows what's at stake: *the throne of David, the return of Messiah, and the reign of God.*

The Covenant in the Last Days

In our time, the headlines scream of conflict, war, and controversy. Missiles rain down, nations threaten, and antisemitism rises again across the globe.

Yet amidst the chaos, the Word of God resounds:

"'Though the mountains be shaken and the hills be removed, yet My unfailing love for you will not be shaken nor My covenant of peace be removed,' says the LORD, Who has compassion on you."

Isaiah 54:10

The preservation of Israel is not rooted in her strength, but in God's **unshakeable covenant**. Her very survival is a signpost to the nations that *God keeps His Word.*

The rebirth of Israel in 1948.[5] The survival of the Six-Day War.[6] The return of Jews from the ends of the earth. All of it points to one truth: **The covenant is still in effect.**

Standing on the Promise

As watchmen, we are not called to be political analysts or passive spectators. We are called to be **intercessors, students of prophecy, and witnesses to the faithfulness of God.**

How should we respond?

- **With honour** toward God's chosen people—not flattery, but reverence

- **With prayer,** standing in the gap for both Israel and the Church

- **With faith,** believing that God will fulfill every word He has spoken

Let the nations rage. Let the fires burn.

The olive tree[7] still stands.

CHAPTER 4

The Rebirth of a Nation

"Who has ever heard of such things? Who has ever seen things like this? Can a country be born in a day or a nation be brought forth in a moment?"

Isaiah 66:8a

The Radio That Changed History[8]

14 May 1948—a date etched in eternity.

In a simple room in Tel Aviv, surrounded by anxious yet resolute leaders, **David Ben-Gurion, the head of the Jewish Agency, stood before a microphone.**[9] As his voice echoed over radios across the land, he proclaimed the establishment of the State of Israel—a declaration that fulfilled a longing 2,000 years old.

"We hereby proclaim the establishment of the Jewish state in Eretz-Israel..."

Outside, tears flowed, prayers rose, and celebration erupted. But beyond the human emotion, something *divine* had taken place. A nation exiled, nearly annihilated, had returned.

No nation in history had suffered so long, been dispersed so far, and yet retained its language, culture, and hope. Only God could write such a story.

This wasn't politics—it was prophecy.

In one day, a scattered people became a sovereign nation. Within hours, five Arab armies declared war. And yet, Israel survived.

Why? Because the Word of the Lord had gone before them.

How? Not by might, nor by power, but by the God who watches over His Word to perform it.

> *"He asked me, 'Son of man, can these bones live?' I said, 'Sovereign LORD, You alone know.'"*
>
> Ezekiel 37:3

The answer came in tanks and tents, in infant cries and IDF uniforms, in prayers at the Western Wall and new immigrants kissing the ground at Ben-Gurion Airport.

The dry bones had begun to rise. The valley of dry bones was rattling.

Flesh was returning. Breath was coming.

This was not just a historical moment—it was a **heavenly announcement:** *God's covenant is alive.*

1. A Promise Delayed, Not Denied

The fall of Jerusalem[10] in AD 70 was not the end, but the beginning of a long night of exile.

Through massacres, inquisitions, ghettos, and gas chambers, the Jewish people endured relentless suffering. The Holocaust[11] was the deepest valley—six million murdered in an industrial-scale genocide. Yet even then, in the smoke of Auschwitz[12] and the ashes of Treblinka,[13] the ancient hope whispered, *"Next year in Jerusalem."*[14]

This hope was not a fantasy. It was rooted in Scripture:

"For I will take you out of the nations; I will gather you from all the countries and bring you back into your own land."

Ezekiel 36:24

"They will live in the land I gave to My servant Jacob, the land where your ancestors lived. They and their children and their children's children will live there forever, and David My servant will be their prince forever."

Ezekiel 37:25

"'I will plant Israel in their own land, never again to be uprooted from the land I have given them,' says the LORD your God."

Amos 9:15

The promise had been delayed by sin, rebellion, and judgment—but it had **not been denied**. God was preparing a moment for His name to be vindicated before all nations.

2. The Significance for the Church

Israel's rebirth is not just a Jewish miracle—it is a message to the Church.

For centuries, many theologians concluded that Israel had been replaced. The Church, they said, was now the "New Israel." But in 1948, God interrupted that narrative.

The fig tree blossomed.

The promises remained.

And Jesus' words in Matthew 24 echoed with fresh power:

> *"Now learn this lesson from the fig tree: As soon as its twigs get tender and its leaves come out, you know that summer is near."*

Matthew 24:32

The rebirth of Israel is a prophetic clock. It is the trumpet blast announcing the nearness of the return of the King. The Church is not meant to be indifferent—we are meant to be **sober, alert, and aligned.**

Art Katz often warned that if the Church misses Israel's significance, she will **miss the nature of God** and **the signs of the times.**

3. Israel: A Living Miracle

By every natural measure, Israel should not exist.

- ✡ A people nearly destroyed, now reborn.

- ✡ A dead language (Hebrew), now a national tongue.

- ✡ A desert, now blossoming with innovation.

- ✡ A people surrounded by enemies, yet undefeated.

Israel is not a symbol of Jewish brilliance—it is a testament to divine faithfulness.

"Therefore say to the Israelites, 'This is what the Sovereign Lord says: It is not for your sake, people of Israel, that I am going to do these things, but for the sake of My holy name.'"

Ezekiel 36:22a

Israel is a mirror. When we look at her rebirth, we see the character of God:

- ✡ A God who keeps covenant

- ✡ A God who remembers mercy

- ✡ A God who prepares His people for the return of His Son

4. The Rebirth and the Watchman

The restoration of Israel is not the end of the story—it's the beginning of the final chapter.

As **watchmen**, we cannot remain neutral or uninformed. We are called to discern the times, to **stand in intercession,** and to **proclaim the nearness of God's Kingdom.**

The rebirth of Israel is a **call to action:**

- ✡ A call to **faith,** because what God has promised, He performs.

- ✡ A call to **intercession,** because the work is not finished.

- ✡ A call to **readiness,** because the King is at the gates.

Let us not be found asleep.

CHAPTER 5

The Church and Israel

Theme:

Understanding the Church's relationship to Israel—past, present, and prophetic

A Grafted Branch in a Sacred Tree

In a sunlit olive grove near Jerusalem, a Jewish farmer crouches beside a weathered tree. In his hands is a wild olive branch—rough, unrefined, but full of potential. With a careful incision, he grafts it into the trunk of a cultivated tree whose roots have dug deep into centuries of sacred soil. He binds the wound, waters the graft, and waits.

Over time, life flows from root to branch. Something new is born—not by erasing the old, but by merging it.

This is the image Paul gave in Romans 11.[15] A divine mystery. A holy union. The Gentile Church grafted into the ancient promises of Israel. Not to replace—but to partake.

1. One Story, Two Peoples, One God

God's redemptive plan didn't begin in Matthew. It began in Genesis—with a man named Abraham. As I mentioned in chapter 3, God made an everlasting covenant with him:

"I will bless those who bless you, and whoever curses you I will curse; and all peoples on earth will be blessed through you."

Genesis 12:3

Israel was chosen—not for privilege, but for purpose. They were called to bear the oracles of God, to carry His presence, and to prepare the way for Messiah.

Jesus, the Son of God, came *as a Jew*. He lived among His people, upheld the Law, and fulfilled the prophetic Scriptures. His disciples were Jewish. The early Church was entirely Jewish—a remnant within Israel that recognised her Messiah.

When Gentiles began to receive salvation, it wasn't a new religion being born. It was the enlargement of the tent. Gentiles were being welcomed into the *already unfolding* story—a covenant extended, not replaced.

"Remember that at that time you were separate from Christ, excluded from citizenship in Israel and foreigners to the covenants of the promise, without hope and without God in the world. But now in Christ Jesus you who once were far away have been brought near by the blood of Christ."

Ephesians 2:12–13

2. The Tragedy of Separation

But somewhere along the road of history, the grafted branch began to boast of its superiority to the root. As the Church became increasingly Gentile, a dangerous shift occurred. A theology emerged that said: "Israel has failed. God has moved on. We are the new Israel."

This doctrine—known as *Replacement Theology*—gained traction. It led to theological arrogance, anti-Semitic persecution, and a tragic distortion of God's heart.

The Holocaust was not birthed in a vacuum. Centuries of Christianised anti-Semitism[16]—sermons that vilified the Jews as "Christ-killers,"[17] laws that segregated them, pogroms[18] that expelled them—laid the groundwork for one of history's greatest horrors.

God's covenant with Israel was not revoked because of failure. He always preserves a remnant. His promises are not fragile.

3. The Church and Israel: Not Competitors, but Co-heirs

Art Katz often said, *"We can't understand the Church unless we understand Israel."*

For too long, the Church has lived as if Israel's rejection of the Messiah was the final word. Some have even claimed that the Church replaced Israel entirely. *But Scripture disagrees.*

"But if some of the branches were broken off, and you, although a wild olive shoot, were grafted in among the others and now share in the nourishing root of the olive tree, do not be arrogant toward the branches. If you are, remember it is not you who support the root, but the root that supports you."

Romans 11:1–18 ESV

Israel is not **discarded**. She is **beloved**, and the Church is not a **replacement**, but a **recipient**—grafted into her story, her Scriptures, her Messiah.

4. Grafted Family: The Mystery of One New Man

Romans 11 reveals a powerful mystery. Israel is the cultivated olive tree. Gentiles are the wild branches. Some Jewish branches were broken off due to unbelief. Gentile believers were grafted in by grace.

Paul warns:

"Then you will say, 'Branches were broken off so that I might be grafted in.' That is true. They were broken off because of their unbelief, but you stand fast through faith. So do not become proud, but fear."

Romans 11:19–20 ESV

We are part of the same tree. We draw from the same root—the covenant God made with Abraham, Isaac, and Jacob. The Church doesn't float on its own authority. It is rooted in Israel's story.

Paul's vision, echoed in Ephesians 2, is that God is creating **"one new man"** out of Jew and Gentile. Not by erasing differences, but by uniting both in the Messiah.

This is not just doctrinal—it's prophetic. When the Church forgets Israel, it loses her prophetic compass. When Israel rejects the Church, she misses the witness of her Messiah. But when both come together under the Lordship of Jesus Christ, the world sees a living testimony of God's power to reconcile what history divided.

5. The Church's Prophetic Responsibility

In these last days, the Church must rediscover her role in relation to Israel. It is not enough to have a sentimental love or political allegiance. We must step into **a prophetic alignment** with God's purposes.

What then is our task?

To Pray

> It is not to gloat but to **intercede**, not to boast but to **bless**. Prayer for Israel is not optional: it is priestly duty.

✡ **To Stand Spiritually**

> To stand with Israel does not mean we need to agree to their every political decision. It is to affirm her place in God's unfolding plan, to stand against anti-Semitism in all forms, and to walk in humility as partakers of her promises.

✡ **To Provoke to Jealousy**

Paul reveals a stunning purpose for the Gentile salvation:

"So I ask, did they stumble in order that they might fall? By no means! Rather, through their trespass salvation has come to the Gentiles, so as to make Israel jealous."

Romans 11:11 ESV

We are called to embody a life so **authentic**, so **Christ-saturated**, that Israel might see **what she was meant to be.**

This means that the Church should be living such radiant, Spirit-filled, cross-bearing life that it causes the Jewish people to look again at Jesus Christ—not as a foreign god, but as *their* Messiah.

6. The Root Still Supports the Branch

The Church is entering days of shaking. To navigate the future, we must be anchored to God's eternal covenants. And Israel—though flawed, often secular, and still in partial blindness—remains central to God's redemptive agenda.

To forget this is to become spiritually orphaned—cut off from the richness of God's history and the trajectory of His future.

A United Calling

The olive tree still grows. The root still nourishes. And every branch—natural and wild—has a role to play in this unfolding drama of redemption.

Let us walk in:

- ✡ **Humility**—never boasting against the root
- ✡ **Gratitude**—for our inclusion in God's covenant
- ✡ **Responsibility**—to pray, stand, and provoke

The story of Israel is not over. And neither is ours.

Scriptures for Further Study:

- ✡ Romans chapters 9, 10, 11

Note:

"Replacement Theology" is discussed more fully in Appendix 1

"Romans 11" is discussed more fully in Appendix 2

PART 3

GOD'S PLAN FOR THE NATIONS

CHAPTER 6

Israel and the Nations

Theme:

The complex relationship between Israel and the nations, and the spiritual implications for the Church and the world; Israel's struggle is not isolated but integrally connected to God's sovereign orchestration of the nations, revealing profound spiritual and prophetic realities.

A World Watching

Israel is often the size of a headline more than the size of a nation. Despite its small geography, **its influence on the global stage is undeniable.** Conflicts in the Middle East can shift economies, provoke UN resolutions, and even sway elections. But the true drama is not geopolitical—it is **prophetic.**

What is unfolding is not merely history or politics. It is **the fulfillment of divine intention**—a redemptive narrative that began with Abraham and will climax with the return of Jesus to Jerusalem.

To understand Israel's place in the world, we must think **biblically, not politically.**

1. God's Sovereignty Over the Nations

The unfolding of history, especially the geopolitical events involving Israel, is under God's meticulous control. In Daniel 2, God reveals to Nebuchadnezzar that He sets up and pulls down kingdoms. Jeremiah 25 and other prophetic passages emphasise that nations are "cups in God's hand," shaped by His divine will.

For the watchman, this truth brings perspective and peace amid turmoil. Though nations rage and conflict intensifies, God's purposes cannot be thwarted. (Isaiah 14:27)

2. Israel's Role Among the Nations

From the very beginning, Israel was chosen for a purpose greater than herself. God's call to Abraham carried a promise that through his descendants, every nation on earth would be blessed. Israel was set apart to reveal God's heart— both a mirror reflecting His character and a messenger carrying His covenant to the world. Though the nations may resist His will, God's faithfulness endures through His people, who are called to shine as His light among them.

"He says: 'It is too small a thing for you to be My servant to restore the tribes of Jacob and bring back those of Israel I have kept. I will also make you a light for the Gentiles, that My salvation may reach to the ends of the earth.'"

Isaiah 49:6

3. The Nations' Response

From Egypt to Babylon, from Rome to modern global powers, **nations have been judged or blessed** based on how they treated Israel.

Today, this continues:

- ✡ **Some bless and support Israel,** aligning with God's covenant purposes.

- ✡ **Others oppose or demonise her,** often under the guise of political justice.

- ✡ **Most remain confused or indifferent,** unable to discern the spiritual undercurrent.

"Why do the nations conspire and the peoples plot in vain? The kings of the earth rise up and the rulers band together against the LORD and against His anointed."

Psalm 2:1–2

Nations will be **held accountable** not just for their policies, but for whether they honoured the God of Israel by respecting His chosen people.

4. The Church and the Nations

The Church is uniquely positioned as **a priesthood among nations**—called to stand in the gap.

Its roles include:

- ✡ **Intercession**—Standing before God on behalf of both Israel and the nations (Ezekiel 22:30)

- ✡ **Advocacy**—Declaring the truth about God's purposes for Israel

- ✡ **Witness**—Calling Gentile nations to repentance and blessing through the gospel

This is not a matter of **favouritism** or nationalism—it is **faithfulness to God's redemptive plan**. The Church must be careful not to repeat the errors of history—where theology replaced Israel rather than embracing her.

5. The Coming Global Shifts

Scripture clearly points to an end-time confrontation involving Israel:

- ✡ Ezekiel 38–39: Nations gather against her—but God intervenes supernaturally.

- ✡ Zechariah 14: The Messiah returns when all nations come against Jerusalem.

- ✡ Matthew 25:31–46: Jesus separates nations based on how they treated "the least of these"—often understood in context as His Jewish brethren.

But from this shaking will come glory:

> *"Many peoples will come and say, 'Come, let us go up to the mountain of the LORD, to the temple of the God of Jacob. He will teach us His ways, so that we may walk in His paths.' The law will go out from Zion, the word of the LORD from Jerusalem."*

Isaiah 2:3

The **gospel will go forth from Jerusalem**, not just to the nations, but through them—as redeemed Gentiles walk in covenant unity with Israel.

6. Hope for the Nations

God's plan has always been global. He chose Israel **for the sake of the nations:**

> *"Then the Lord said, 'Shall I hide from Abraham what I am about to do? Abraham will surely become a great and powerful nation, and all nations on earth will be blessed through him.'"*

Genesis 18:17–18

- ✡ Every tribe, tongue, people, and nation will stand before His throne (Revelation 7:9)

- ✡ The earth shall be full of the knowledge of the Lord (Isaiah 11:9)

There is hope even for nations that have failed—**if they repent** and align with God's heart.

Engaging the Nations Spiritually

Israel is not just a natural nation. It is a **spiritual litmus test** for the world. Our response reveals **who we truly serve**: the God of Abraham, Isaac, and Jacob—or the systems of this world.

Art Katz, a key spiritual mentor for many, taught that believers cannot be neutral or passive. Instead, they must actively discern the signs of the times and engage with Israel's struggle in faith.

How Should We Respond?

✡ **Pray** for nations to come into alignment with God's plan

✡ **Bless** Israel intentionally and scripturally

✡ **Disciple** leaders with a prophetic worldview

✡ **Proclaim** the gospel boldly—to Jew and Gentile (Romans 1:16)

✡ **Live as Watchmen and Witnesses**: Remain alert, warn and prepare for Christ's return with readiness and faith.

✡ **Reject Anti-Semitism and Division**: Repentance for the Church's failures regarding the Jewish people is vital. The Church must stand firmly against anti-Semitism and promote unity.

✡ **Bridge** reconciliation between the Church and Israel (Matthew 5:9)

This is not optional. This is the mandate of the watchmen.

The role of the Church transcends politics and culture—it is a divine mandate to partner with God's plan for Israel and the nations. Standing with Israel means participating in the unfolding drama of redemption that affects the entire world.

Scriptures for Further Study:

✡ Daniel 2 — God's sovereignty over kingdoms

✡ Jeremiah 25 — The nations are cups in God's hand

✡ Isaiah 14:27 — *"For the LORD Almighty has purposed, and who can thwart Him? His hand is stretched out, and who can turn it back?"*

✡ Ezekiel 38–39 — Nations gather against Israel but God intervenes supernaturally.

✡ Zechariah 14 — The Lord comes and reigns

✡ Matthew 25:31–46 — The sheep and the goats

✡ Revelation 7:9 — *"After this I looked, and there before me was a great multitude that no one could count, from every nation, tribe, people and language, standing before the throne and before the Lamb. They were wearing white robes and were holding palm branches in their hands."*

✡ Isaiah 11:9b — *"For the earth will be filled with the knowledge of the LORD as the waters cover the sea."*

✡ Romans 1:16 — *"For I am not ashamed of the gospel, because it is the power of God that brings salvation to everyone who believes: first to the Jew, then to the Gentile."*

✡ Matthew 5:9 — *"Blessed are the peacemakers, for they will be called children of God."*

CHAPTER 7

The Hope of Restoration —
Israel and the Church's Future

Theme:

Encouragement and assurance for believers amidst Israel's modern struggles and God's ultimate victory.

"'But I will restore you to health and heal your wounds,' declares the LORD, 'because you are called an outcast, Zion for whom no one cares.'"

Jeremiah 30:17

"'For I know the plans I have for you,' declares the Lord, 'plans to prosper you and not to harm you, plans to give you hope and a future.'"

Jeremiah 29:11

The Wounded People, the Faithful God

In my travels, I have seen the weight of history on the faces of the Jewish people. Some carry it with dignity. Others, with deep scepticism—toward God, religion, and even hope. And who can blame them? The Holocaust is not ancient history. Pogroms, inquisitions, forced conversions—these aren't distant legends, but living memory.

Yet, in the midst of these wounds, **God speaks restoration.** Not merely consolation, but **resurrection.**

> *"He asked me, 'Son of man, can these bones live?' I said, 'Sovereign LORD, You alone know.'"*

> Ezekiel 37:3

And the answer came:

> *"Then He said to me, 'Prophesy to these bones and say to them, 'Dry bones, hear the word of the LORD! This is what the Sovereign LORD says to these bones: I will make breath enter you, and you will come to life. I will attach tendons to you and make flesh come upon you and cover you with skin; I will put breath in you, and you will come to life. Then you will know that I am the LORD.'"*

> Ezekiel 37:4–6

This is not poetry. It is **prophecy.** It is **destiny.** It is the heartbeat of a covenant-keeping God who does not abandon His purposes.

Restoration is Spiritual Before it is National

While the headlines focus on wars, politics, and territory, the deeper issue is **spiritual estrangement**. Israel's ultimate restoration is not merely a matter of borders or treaties—it is about **her heart turning back to her God.**

> *"And I will give you a new heart, and a new spirit I will put within you. And I will remove the heart of stone from your flesh and give you a heart of flesh. And I will put My Spirit within you, and cause you to walk in My statutes and be careful to obey My rules. You shall dwell in the land that I gave to your fathers, and you shall be My people, and I will be your God."*

Ezekiel 36:26–28 ESV

The modern State of Israel is a **miraculous fulfillment**—but it is not the conclusion. It is the **beginning of the return.** The return to land precedes the return to God.

And just as Ezekiel prophesied, the **bones come together first**—structure without breath. But then, the **Spirit comes,** and life floods the corpse of national identity with divine purpose.

The Church's Future is Tied to Israel's Awakening

Many Christians long for revival, for the return of Christ, for a pure and radiant Bride. But few realise that **these things are tied to Israel's awakening.**

"For I tell you, you will not see Me again until you say, 'Blessed is He who comes in the name of the Lord.'"

Matthew 23:39

The Lord ties His return to **Israel's recognition** of Him. The Church's mission, then, is not just global evangelism—but specifically to the Jew first (Romans 1:16). Not out of strategy, but **because this is God's order.** Israel's restoration means **resurrection power** for the entire Church.

"For if their rejection brought reconciliation to the world, what will their acceptance be but life from the dead?"

Romans 11:15

The Coming Kingdom: New Heaven, New Earth

As we look ahead, the hope of restoration bursts beyond Israel and even beyond the Church—it **encompasses creation itself.**

"See, I will create new heavens and a new earth."

Isaiah 65:17a

"He will wipe every tear from their eyes. There will be no more death or mourning or crying or pain, for the old order of things has passed away."

Revelation 21:4

God's redemptive plan is total: from Eden's loss to Zion's glory, from broken bodies to resurrected saints. The new Jerusalem will come—not as a fantasy, but as **the fulfilled dream of both Testaments.**

Jerusalem: The Clock of Prophecy

Walk through the streets of Jerusalem, and you're walking through prophecy. You can feel the tension—religions clashing, nations watching, spirits brooding. Jerusalem is not just a capital—it is a **timepiece.**

When you see Israel regathered (Isaiah 11:12), Jerusalem under Jewish control (Luke 21:24), and the nations turning against her—you know time is short.

Jesus said: *"So also, when you see all these things, you know that He is near, at the very gates."* (Matthew 24:33 ESV)

The Tribulation and the Purification of Israel

Daniel, Zechariah, and Revelation speak of a coming time of great tribulation. Israel will suffer—but through the fire, a **remnant**[19] will emerge who see their Messiah.

This will not be merely a revival—it will be a **revelation**. The veil will be lifted. The One whom they thought was foreign will be recognised as family.

> *"Though the fig tree does not bud and there are no grapes on the vines, though the olive crop fails and the fields produce no food, though there are no sheep in the pen and no cattle in the stalls, yet I will rejoice in the LORD, I will be joyful in God my Saviour."*

Habakkuk 3:17–18

The Remnant of Israel and the Church — God's Faithful Few

In the midst of turmoil, widespread unfaithfulness, and conflict, God always preserves a faithful remnant—a humble people who remain steadfast and cling to Him. This remnant is not just a theological idea but a living reality that runs through the history of Israel and the Church alike. Their existence assures us that God's purposes are never thwarted, even when circumstances seem bleak.

Hope for the Future— Dawn on the Horizon

The ancient city of Jerusalem, despite enduring cycles of turmoil and conflict, shines with a promise rooted in God's unchanging faithfulness. This hope transcends current struggles because it rests on the eternal character of God —a God who keeps His covenant and fulfills His promises.

1. God's Faithfulness Through the Ages

✡ From the call of Abraham, God has remained faithful to His covenant people.

✡ Despite periods of exile (Deuteronomy 28:64–67), persecution, and war, Israel remains central in God's redemptive plan.

✡ God's promises to restore and bless Israel are sure and unfolding according to His perfect timing (Psalm 105:8–11).

2. The Promise of Restoration

✡ **Peace and Justice:** Isaiah 2:4 — Signifies an era of lasting peace and the end of warfare, as people will no longer fight or train for war.

✡ **Worship of the Nations:** Psalm 87 — Celebrates the nations gathering to Zion.

✡ **Messianic Reign:** Jeremiah 23:5–6 — The righteous Branch, the coming King.

These prophetic assurances fuel the hope that, one day, the world will be reconciled and restored under God's just rule.

3. Our Hope as Watchmen

✡ Our hope is rooted in the power of God to redeem and save (Ephesians 1:18–20)

✡ We anticipate the coming Kingdom of God where peace and righteousness will reign supreme (Daniel

7:13–14)

✡ We are called to actively participate in God's unfolding story, praying and standing as watchmen for Jerusalem and the world.

4. Living in Expectation

✡ Keep your eyes fixed on Jesus, the author and perfecter of faith (Hebrews 12:2)

✡ Stand firm and courageous in the face of trials, knowing your labour is not in vain (1 Corinthians 15:58)

✡ Boldly proclaim the hope found in Israel's Messiah—Jesus Christ (Romans 15:12–13)

5. The Final Victory

✡ **Light Over Darkness:** John 1:5 — A message of hope that even in the darkest times the light of God's truth and presence will ultimately prevail

✡ **Purposeful Life:** Romans 8:28 — God works all things for good

✡ **Eternal Peace:** Revelation 21:1–4 — New heaven and new earth, no more suffering or death

This certainty of victory sustains the watchman's heart and fuels perseverance.

Hope That Sustains

In a world often marked by uncertainty and conflict, the hope God provides is unshakable. We live not by sight but by faith (2 Corinthians 5:7), moving forward with courage, faith, and relentless hope, confident that God's promises will be fulfilled.

Hope Beyond Conflict

Despite the nations' turmoil and resistance, the final chapter of history is God's to write. The watchman's role is to remain vigilant, prayerful, and active—holding fast to hope while advocating for peace and justice.

"Watchman, lift your eyes and see—the dawn is coming."

The Church in the Final Hour

This is not the time for comfort, entertainment, or escapism. This is the time to **watch**, **pray**, and **prepare**.

The true Church must:

- ✡ Be awake — spiritually discerning, prophetically alert

- ✡ Be **ready** — in holiness, faith, and love

- ✡ Be **engaged** — boldly preaching, especially to Israel

"For the grace of God has appeared that offers salvation to all people. It teaches us to say 'No' to ungodliness and worldly passions, and to live self-controlled, upright and godly lives in this present age, while we wait for the blessed hope—the appearing of the glory of our great God and Saviour, Jesus Christ, who gave Himself for us to redeem us from all wickedness and to purify for Himself a people that are His very own, eager to do what is good."

Titus 2:11–14

The Church that is **married to this world** will not be ready for the One to come. But those who live as **watchmen** will recognise the signs and cry, *"Maranatha!"*

Maranatha: Come, Lord Jesus!

This chapter ends where the age itself will end—not with fear, but with a **longing cry**.

Let the Spirit and the Bride say: **Come!** (Revelation 22:17)

Let the Jewish people awaken to their Messiah.

Let the Church return to her calling.

Let the nations tremble at His coming.

Let the hope of restoration become the fuel for endurance.

Let the final cry rise from the earth like incense from a burning altar:

Maranatha! Come, Lord Jesus!

Scriptures for Further Study:

✡ Isaiah 11:12 — *"He will raise a banner for the nations and gather the exiles of Israel; He will assemble the scattered people of Judah from the four quarters of the earth."*

✡ Luke 21:24b — *"Jerusalem will be trampled on by the Gentiles until the times of the Gentiles are fulfilled."*

✡ Psalm 105:8–11 — God's covenant remembered through generations

✡ Isaiah 2:4 — *"He will judge between the nations and will settle disputes for many peoples. They will beat their swords into ploughshares and their spears into pruning hooks. Nation will not take up sword against nation, nor will they train for war anymore."*

✡ Jeremiah 23:5–6 — The righteous Branch and King to come

✡ Ephesians 1:18–20 — Hope and power through the Spirit

✡ Daniel 7:13–14 — *"In my vision at night I looked, and there before me was one like a Son of Man, coming with the clouds of heaven. He approached the Ancient of Days and was led into His presence. He was given authority, glory and sovereign power; all nations and peoples of every language worshipped Him. His dominion is an everlasting dominion that will not pass away, and His kingdom is one that will never be destroyed."*

✡ Hebrews 12:2 — *"Fixing our eyes on Jesus, the pioneer and perfecter of faith. For the joy set before Him He endured the cross, scorning its shame, and sat down at the right hand of the throne of God."*

✡ 1 Corinthians 15:58 — *"Therefore, my dear brothers and sisters, stand firm. Let nothing move you. Always give yourselves fully to the work of the Lord, because you know that your labour in the Lord is not in vain."*

✡ Romans 15:12–13 — Hope and joy through faith

✡ John 1:5 — *"The light shines in the darkness, and the darkness has not overcome it."*

✡ Revelation 22:17 — *"The Spirit and the Bride say, 'Come!' And let the one who hears say, 'Come!' Let the one who is thirsty come; and let the one who wishes take the free gift of the water of life."*

Note:

"The Remnant" is discussed more fully in Appendix 3

PART 4

SPIRITUAL CONFLICT
AND THE WATCHMAN'S ROLE

CHAPTER 8

War in the Land

Theme:

Understanding the spiritual and geopolitical dimensions of Israel's current conflicts.

"For our struggle is not against flesh and blood, but against the rulers, against the authorities, against the powers of this dark world and against the spiritual forces of evil in the heavenly realms."

Ephesians 6:12

Sirens in the Night

In the stillness of a Tel Aviv night, sirens wail. Children are ushered into bomb shelters. Moments later, explosions echo as Israel's Iron Dome defends the skies. This is not fiction. It is the rhythm of life in Israel—where moments of peace are always under threat.

Behind every act of violence or international controversy lies a deeper reality: **a spiritual battle.** This isn't merely geopolitical—it's a collision of kingdoms.

1. A Land at the Crossroads

Israel is only a small piece of land, yet the entire world watches her. Why? Because **Israel is not just a geographical location—she is a spiritual epicentre.** From her came the Scriptures, the covenants, the Messiah.

She is:

- Surrounded by terror groups
- Criticised by nations
- Longing for the fulfillment of God's promises

2. The Current Crisis: A Snapshot

October 2023[20] and Beyond

The brutal Hamas assault shook Israel to its core—igniting a war that affects civilians, soldiers, and the entire region.

Rising Anti-Semitism

Across the globe, anti-Semitism is rising again—a spiritual hatred with ancient roots.

Haman's desire to annihilate the Jews echoes this age-old hatred.

"Yet having learned who Mordecai's people were, he scorned the idea of killing only Mordecai. Instead Haman looked for a way to destroy all Mordecai's people, the Jews, throughout the whole kingdom of Xerxes."

Esther 3:6

"If the world hates you, keep in mind that it hated Me first."

John 15:18

Internal Division

Even within Israel, divisions deepen—religious vs. secular, political left vs. right. Yet, often, crisis brings a divine reset.

3. What Does the Bible Say About This?

The Bible may not mention modern armies or political names, but it speaks clearly of the dynamics at play:

- ✡ Zechariah 12:3 — All nations will feel the weight of Jerusalem

- ✡ Psalm 83 — A prayer for the protection and deliverance of Israel from a powerful coalition of nations that conspire to destroy them and erase their name from the earth

- ✡ Matthew 24:6–8 — signs of end times

These prophecies don't lead to fear—they reveal that history is headed toward a **divine climax.**

- ✡ Zechariah 14:2–4 — A future day when nations will attack Jerusalem but God will then intervene and fight against the attackers and establish His eternal kingdom

- ✡ Daniel 12:1 — A time of distress for Israel like no other

- ✡ Isaiah 60:1–2 — Darkness will cover the earth, but God's light will rise on Zion

4. Spiritual Warfare, Not Just Political

Every earthly war has a spiritual war behind it. The enemy seeks to destroy what God has chosen.

- ✡ Israel is central because of God's covenants

- ✡ Satan resists her destiny because the Messiah will return to Jerusalem

5. The Role of the Watchman in Times of War

In such days, the Church cannot remain neutral or ignorant. God is calling His people to watch, pray, and proclaim truth:

- ✡ **Watchmen are awake** to the times

- ✡ **They pray with insight,** not mere sentiment

- ✡ **They speak boldly** in a sea of lies

- ✡ **They stand in the gap,** even when misunderstood

Between the Headlines and Heaven

These events are not random. God is sounding the alarm. War in Israel is not the conclusion—it is a sign pointing us to urgency, repentance, and hope.

Our Response Should Be:

- ✡ **Prayer** — always the first response
- ✡ **Hope** (Romans 15:13) — rooted in God's promises
- ✡ **Compassion** — for Jews and Arabs alike (Luke 10:33)

The Battle Belongs to the Lord

Though Israel faces a physical war, **the true battle is spiritual, and the victory is already written.** As watchmen, we stand not as commentators but as participants—praying, interceding, and proclaiming that the **King is coming.**

Scriptures for Further Study:

- ✡ Zechariah 12:3 — *"On that day, when all the nations of the earth are gathered against her, I will make Jerusalem an immovable rock for all the nations. All who try to move it will injure themselves."*

- ✡ Romans 9:4–5 — *"The people of Israel. Theirs is the adoption to sonship; theirs the divine glory, the covenants... and the promises. Theirs are the patriarchs, and from them is traced the human ancestry of the Messiah, who is God over all, forever praised! Amen."*

✡ Daniel 12:1 — *"At that time Michael, the great prince who protects your people, will arise. There will be a time of distress such as has not happened from the beginning of nations until then. But at that time your people—everyone whose name is found written in the book—will be delivered."*

✡ Isaiah 60:1–2 — *"Arise, shine, for your light has come, and the glory of the LORD rises upon you. See, darkness covers the earth and thick darkness is over the peoples, but the LORD rises upon you and His glory appears over you."*

✡ Romans 15:13 — *"May the God of hope fill you with all joy and peace as you trust in Him, so that you may overflow with hope by the power of the Holy Spirit."*

✡ Psalm 2:1–6 — Describes the futility of human rulers rebelling against God and His chosen king, who is identified as God's anointed Son, Jesus Christ

✡ Habakkuk 1:5 — *"Look at the nations and watch—and be utterly amazed. For I am going to do something in your days that you would not believe even if you were told."*

✡ Romans 11:26 — *"And in this way all Israel will be saved. As it is written: 'The deliverer will come from Zion, He will turn godlessness away from Jacob.'"*

CHAPTER 9

The Spiritual Battle for Jerusalem

Theme:

Exploring the intense spiritual warfare surrounding Jerusalem and its significance in God's redemptive plan

"For the LORD your God is a consuming fire, a jealous God."

Deuteronomy 4:24

The City on a Hill

Jerusalem is not just a geographical location; it is a spiritual epicentre. Perched atop the hills of Judah, it has been called the "City of Peace"—yet it has seen more bloodshed than nearly any other place on earth. From David's conquest to the Babylonian exile, from Roman occupation to the modern conflict between nations, the battle for Jerusalem rages on.

But behind the political headlines and military escalations lies a deeper war—**a cosmic struggle**. The spiritual significance of this city is unparalleled. Every attempt to divide, desecrate, or dominate it is ultimately rooted in **spiritual resistance to God's will**.

1. Why Jerusalem?

Jerusalem is targeted because it is central to God's purposes:

- ✡ The dwelling place of God's name — 1 Kings 11:36

- ✡ The spiritual capital of the world — Psalm 48:2

- ✡ The city of Christ's return and reign — Zechariah 14:4

Satan does not waste his energy on what is irrelevant. His focus on Jerusalem is a recognition of its eternal significance. **To destabilise Jerusalem is to attack the throne of the coming King.**

2. Biblical Evidence of Spiritual Conflict

Scripture reveals the invisible war raging over Jerusalem:

- ✡ Spiritual resistance to God's work — Zechariah 3:1

- ✡ Angelic involvement in protecting God's purpose — Psalm 34:7

- ✡ Heaven's response to Jerusalem's plight: When Daniel fasted for understanding, he was told by the angel that **spiritual princes** opposed him (Daniel 10:13). The same kind of **territorial spirits** still oppose the unfolding of God's will in Jerusalem today.

3. Modern Warfare Reflects Spiritual Realities

The visible conflict—missiles, protests, political negotiations—is only **the outer layer**. Underneath it is a deeper resistance to God's redemptive plan:

- ✡ Every rocket fired is a distraction from the Prince of Peace

- ✡ Every diplomatic scheme that ignores God's covenant land is a counterfeit solution

- ✡ Every act of terrorism or desecration is an attempt to unseat God's authority

But the Church has not been left powerless. We are armed with the **weapons of righteousness**—intercession, proclamation, and spiritual authority.

4. The Church's Role in the Battle

To be ignorant of Jerusalem's battle is to be **disconnected from God's heartbeat**. As Art Katz often emphasised, to love God is to love what He loves—and He **loves Jerusalem**.

Our call is to:

- ✡ **Pray** — persistently and prophetically

- ✡ **Declare** — God's unchanging promises over the city

- ✡ **Stand** — against deception and spiritual compromise

- ✡ **Intercede** — for salvation to come to the Jewish people (Romans 10:1)

Jerusalem's restoration is not just about politics or peace agreements—it is about the **return of the King.**

5. Victory Is Certain

The outcome of this battle is already written:

> *"For the LORD Almighty has purposed, and who can thwart Him? His hand is stretched out, and who can turn it back?"*

> Isaiah 14:27

> *"Then the LORD will go out and fight against those nations, as He fights on a day of battle."*

> Zechariah 14:3

> *"I saw heaven standing open and there before me was a white horse, whose rider is called Faithful and True. With justice He judges and wages war. His eyes are like blazing fire, and on His head are many crowns. He has a name written on Him that no one knows but He Himself. He is dressed in a robe dipped in blood, and His name is the Word of God. The armies of heaven were following Him, riding on white horses and dressed in fine linen, white and clean.*

> Revelation 19:11–14

Jerusalem will one day be **the joy of all the earth,** a city of righteousness, peace, and the throne of Messiah.

The battle is real. The hour is late. But God is raising up **watchmen who see,** who weep, and who war—not with weapons of the world, but with **truth, prayer, and prophetic courage.**

How Should We Respond?

- ✡ Join the prayer movement[21] for Jerusalem's peace

- ✡ Engage in informed spiritual warfare[22]

- ✡ Walk in purity and authority as kingdom ambassadors

- ✡ Live with confidence in God's unshakable purpose

Scriptures for Further Study:

- ✡ Psalm 48:1–2 — *"Beautiful in its loftiness, the joy of the whole earth ... is Mount Zion, the city of the Great King."*

- ✡ 1 Kings 11:36 — God chooses Jerusalem to bear His Name

- ✡ Zechariah 14:4 — Messiah returns to the Mount of Olives

- ✡ Zechariah 3:1 — *"Then he showed me Joshua the high priest standing before the angel of the LORD, and Satan standing at his right side to accuse him."*

- ✡ Psalm 34:7 — *"The angel of the LORD encamps around those who fear Him, and He delivers them."*

- ✡ Daniel 10:13 — *"But the prince of the Persian kingdom resisted me twenty-one days. Then Michael, one of the chief princes, came to help me, because I was detained there with the king of Persia."*

- ✡ Romans 10:1 — *"Brothers and sisters, my heart's desire and prayer to God for the Israelites is that they may be saved."*

CHAPTER 10

Spiritual Warfare — Standing in the Gap

"I looked for someone among them who would build up the wall and stand before Me in the gap on behalf of the land so I would not have to destroy it, but I found no one."

Ezekiel 22:30

"He saw that there was no man, and wondered that there was no intercessor; Therefore His own arm brought salvation for Him; And His own righteousness, it sustained Him."

Isaiah 59:16 NKJV

The Watchman's Spiritual Mandate

The watchman's role is not passive. It is a divine summons to engage spiritually. Watchmen don't merely observe destruction; they fight against it through intercession. They stand between judgment and mercy, appealing to God on behalf of a people and a land.

The Power of Intercessory Prayer

Prayer is not an escape from reality—it is the **primary battlefield** where spiritual authority is exercised. Through prayer, the Church aligns itself with God's redemptive will for Israel and the nations.

Art Katz taught:

> *"Prayer that moves God must be born of God. It comes from His burden, not our agendas. It is priestly, sacrificial, and costly."*

> *"The effective, fervent prayer of a righteous man avails much."*

James 5:16b NKJV

> *"Likewise the Spirit also helps in our weaknesses. For we do not know what we should pray for as we ought, but the Spirit Himself makes intercession for us with groanings which cannot be uttered."*

Romans 8:26 NKJV

Standing in the Gap

To stand in the gap means to **take up the burden of intercession,** even when others are indifferent or unaware. It is a posture of **identification** and **sacrificial love,** as seen in Moses and Paul.

Scripture References:

- ✡ Exodus 32:11–14 — Moses pleaded with God to spare Israel.

- ✡ Romans 9:1–3 — Paul was willing to be *"cut off"* for the sake of his people.

- ✡ Isaiah 53:12 — *"And He bore the sin of many and made intercession for the transgressors."*

Art Katz said:

"True intercession does not come cheaply. It is agony. It is the travail of God expressed through His people."

The Armour of God

Spiritual warfare demands that the watchman be fully equipped. Paul outlines the armour in Ephesians 6, each piece essential for battle:

- ✡ Belt of Truth — Integrity and grounding in God's reality

- ✡ Breastplate of Righteousness — Right standing and holy living

- ✡ Shoes of the Gospel of Peace — Readiness and proclamation

- ✡ Shield of Faith — Protection from lies and fiery trials

- ✡ Helmet of Salvation — Guarding the mind with eternal hope

- ✡ Sword of the Spirit — Declaring and wielding the Word of God

Arne Hamilton, an experienced prayer minister and a dear friend of ours, has this to say about the 'armour of God':

"Any Jewish person reading Paul's letter to the Ephesians would have known he was referring to the kiss of God by what he picked for the armour—righteousness, peace, truth and faith—which are found in God's kiss in Psalm 85.

The Hebrew word for putting on armour is the same as for kissing. The armour of God is actually His kiss."[23]

Daily Application Tip:

Pray on the armour every day. Ask for God's kiss on you and your loved ones. It's not symbolic—it's survival.

Prayer as Prophetic Action

When watchmen pray, they are **not just asking—they are proclaiming.** They speak what God has said and what He will yet do. Their intercession becomes a prophetic act: **calling down heaven into earth's affairs.**

Scripture References:

✡ Jeremiah 1:10 — *"See, today I appoint you over nations and kingdoms to uproot and tear down, to destroy and overthrow, to build and to plant."*

✡ Job 22:28 NKJV — *"You will also declare a thing, and it will be established for you; So light will shine on your ways."*

The Watchman's Warfare

The Church cannot afford to be prayerless or disengaged. The warfare over Israel is **real**, **present**, and **spiritually strategic**. God is calling believers to rise as intercessors—not spectators. Prayer is not optional—it is the battleground where destinies are shaped.

Understanding the Battle

The opposition to Israel's calling is not merely geopolitical—it is spiritual. The forces of darkness recognise the prophetic role of Israel in God's plan and seek to disrupt it. Paul wrote that the real battle for Christians is not against people but against spiritual rulers, authorities, and cosmic powers in the heavenly realms. (Ephesians 6:12)

For so many years I took this truth seriously and joined the intercessory groups that would challenge these spiritual beings and went around binding them in their many forms of manifestations in people's lives. My wife and I thought we were doing an incredible work for the kingdom of God until we had a wake-up call and began to have a real understanding of the battle we're in.

God in His mercy led us to the book of **John Paul Jackson**, *Needless Casualties of War*,[24] that changed the way we pray and intercede. These are some of the truths taken from his book and as you read this part, we pray that you will have that revelation, too.

From: *Needless Casualties of War* by John Paul Jackson

Introduction: The Unseen War

There is a spiritual war raging around us—a war that affects families, cities, and nations. As believers, we are not called to passivity but to active engagement. However, *Needless Casualties of War* reveals a sobering truth: many believers are suffering unnecessary defeat in spiritual warfare because of misguided zeal and a lack of divine order.

Key Principle #1: Authority Flows from Alignment

In the spiritual realm, **authority is not seized—it is delegated.** We cannot bypass divine order or assignments. John Paul Jackson warns against spiritual trespassing: praying or warring in realms we were not authorised to engage. This is not fear-driven caution; it's reverent obedience.

- ✡ **Illustration:** A private in the army cannot command a battalion. Similarly, believers must stay within their God-given jurisdiction in spiritual warfare.

- ✡ **Biblical Example:** The seven sons of Sceva (Acts 19:13–16) tried to cast out demons "in the name of Jesus whom Paul preaches" and were overpowered because they lacked true authority.

Key Principle #2:
Warfare Must Flow from Intimacy

Spiritual warfare must begin with relational intimacy and alignment to God's order.

The safest place in warfare is under God's shadow, not on the frontlines we were never sent to.

The greatest warriors are the closest friends of God. True authority is birthed in the secret place. Jesus only did what He saw the Father doing (John 5:19), and so must we.

- ✡ **Intimacy builds clarity.** If we are unsure what or whom to war against, we must return to the place of worship, surrender, and listening.

- ✡ **Worship is warfare:** It realigns our spirit, dethrones fear, and enthrones God.

Key Principle #3:
Covering and Community Matter

We are part of a **spiritual body.** Lone rangers in spiritual warfare become easy targets. Accountability, spiritual covering in prayer, and corporate intercession create a shield of protection.

- ✡ *Needless Casualties of War* includes stories of intercessors who suffered sickness, family crises, and financial loss—not because spiritual warfare isn't real, but because it was *presumed* without proper prayer covering or counsel.

"When we step outside our jurisdiction, we step outside our protection."

Conclusion: The Call to Wise Warfare

We are called to be warriors—but wise ones. Passion must be tempered by revelation. Warfare must be birthed in worship. And engagement must be directed by the Spirit.

Let us:

1. Stay within our assigned sphere.

2. Cultivate intimacy with Jesus.

3. Submit to spiritual authority and community.

4. Be led, not driven, in battle.

Prayer:

"Lord, train our hands for war and our fingers for battle (Psalm 144:1). Deliver us from presumptuous warfare. Teach us to war with wisdom, intimacy, and holy fear. May we never fight battles You didn't assign us. And may we move only under Your authority, for Your glory. Amen."

Anne Hamilton has this to say about Spiritual Warfare:

✡ Jude, the brother of Jesus, warns us about dealing with fallen angelic powers, saying: *"Even the archangel Michael, when he disputed with the devil... did not presume to bring a slanderous charge against him, but said, 'The Lord rebuke you!'"* (Jude 1:9 BSB)[25]

✡ Jesus cast out low-level demons and rebuked higher-level ones. And the principle given to us by Jude and Peter (for our own safety) is to ask the Lord to rebuke them, not do it ourselves. (2 Peter 2:10–11)

I think it's that simple. When we've got a problem with angelic bullies, we aren't supposed to fight them (except with the Word of God). We're to limit ourselves to that. And when they've gone too far, as bullies are apt to do, we're supposed to ask our heavenly Dad to tell them off.[26]

✡ *"On this rock I will My church, and the gates of Hades will not overcome it. I will give you the keys of the kingdom of heaven; whatever you bind on earth will be bound in heaven, and whatever you loose on earth will be loosed in heaven."* (Matthew 16:18–19)

Spiritual warfare today loosely bandies about the word *"bind"* without understanding that it's about legal restraint—and that we need to be exceedingly careful how we exercise it.[27]

✡ When we expect "all authority" means we can bind whatever spirits we like, regardless of what is said about them in God's Word, we fail to understand what it means to be *under* authority and how to legitimately exercise it.[28]

Scriptures for Further Study:

✡ Daniel 9:3–4 — Daniel interceded for Israel with fasting, confession, and earnest prayer.

✡ Revelation 12:17 — The dragon makes war against the "rest of her offspring"—those who keep God's commands and hold on to Jesus.

✡ Ephesians 6:10–18 — The full armour of God

✡ Acts 19:13–16 — The seven sons of Sceva casting demons out of a man

✡ John 5:19 — *"Jesus gave them this answer: 'Very truly I tell you, the Son can do nothing by Himself; He can do only what He sees His Father doing, because whatever the Father does the Son also does.'"*

✡ 2 Peter 2:10–11 — *"This is especially true of those who follow the corrupt desire of the flesh and despise authority. Bold and arrogant, they are not afraid to heap abuse on celestial beings; yet even angels, although they are stronger and more powerful, do not heap abuse on such beings when bringing judgment on them from the Lord."*

✡ Jude 1:9 — *"But even the archangel Michael, when he was disputing with the devil about the body of Moses, did not himself dare to condemn him for slander but said, 'The Lord rebuke you!'"*

CHAPTER 11

Practical Steps for Watchmen — How to Engage with Israel's Struggle Today

Understanding Israel's prophetic significance and embracing the calling of watchmen is essential—but what does it mean to live it out daily? How do we translate passion and theology into faithful, practical engagement?

This chapter offers six actionable steps that believers can adopt to stand firm, pray faithfully, and serve effectively in this critical hour.

1. Cultivate a Lifestyle of Prayer

Prayer is the heartbeat of a watchman. It is the spiritual connection that fuels vigilance and intercession.

> ✡ **Set a rhythm:** Establish dedicated daily times to

pray specifically for Israel—early morning, noon, or evening—wherever you can consistently meet with God.

✡ **Pray strategically:** Focus on key needs such as peace in Jerusalem and the Middle East, protection over leaders and citizens, and spiritual awakening in the Church globally.

✡ **Intercede boldly:** Lift up those in ministry in Israel, Jewish believers, and the global Body of Christ.

✡ **Seek revelation:** Ask the Holy Spirit to open your eyes to God's heart and unfolding plans, enabling you to pray with insight and power.

2. Study God's Word on Israel

Knowledge shapes prayer and action.

✡ **Dive into Scripture:** Engage deeply with passages about Israel's covenant, promises, and prophetic destiny (e.g., Genesis 12, Romans 11, Ezekiel 37).

✡ **Use trustworthy resources:** Supplement your study with devotionals, commentaries, and teaching from reputable teachers who uphold biblical orthodoxy.

✡ **Grow in understanding:** Understanding the spiritual significance behind current events equips you to pray and witness with authority.

3. Stand in Unity with the Body of Christ

Watchmen do not stand alone.

- ✡ **Find community:** Join or form prayer groups focused on Israel, locally or online, where you can share insights, pray in agreement, and encourage one another.

- ✡ **Tap into networks:** There are many intercessory networks worldwide specifically devoted to praying for Israel and the Church's role in the end times.

- ✡ **Experience strength in numbers:** Corporate prayer unleashes a powerful spiritual dynamics—God's presence. Jesus promised:

"For where two or three gather in My name, there am I with them."

Matthew 18:20

4. Support Israel Practically

Prayer must be accompanied by action.

- ✡ **Educate others:** Share what you learn about Israel's biblical significance with your church and social circles, helping others to see the spiritual dimension.

- ✡ **Visit Israel:** If possible, travel to Israel to walk the land, meet believers, and pray on-site. Firsthand experience can deepen our passion and understanding.

✡ **Encourage ministries:** Support organizations ministering to Jewish communities and those promoting peace and reconciliation.

On a personal note, several years ago when we were still living in Australia, my wife and I joined an organisation that hosts Israeli travellers. It's called HITinternational.[29] We were able to host several groups of these travellers or tourists before COVID and it was such an enriching experience.

When these Israeli travellers entered our home, it was more than just offering a place to stay—it was opening our hearts to a unique encounter. They were not believers of Yeshua as their Messiah, yet they carried with them the story of Israel, a living testimony of a people whose history has shaped nations and continues to carry deep meaning for us today.

From the very first meal together, walls came down. Around the table we shared food, laughter, and stories—about life in Israel, its landscapes and traditions, and about our own journey here at home. The conversations were full of curiosity on both sides, and we quickly discovered that kindness and respect speak a language everyone understands.

Though our beliefs were different, hospitality became the common ground. Our home transformed into more than four walls—it became a sanctuary of connection. We realised that welcoming others is not about convincing or debating, but about honouring, serving, and creating space for genuine friendship.

As we listened to their stories, we were reminded of God's faithfulness to Israel across the centuries. And even though we came from different perspectives, we felt the Lord's smile over our time together. In extending welcome, we were the ones deeply blessed—our faith was stirred, our understanding was broadened, and our hearts were enriched.

By the time they left, our home felt fuller—not just with memories, but with the joy of having shared in something larger than ourselves. Hosting them became a small glimpse of God's greater plan: a day when all nations will sit together at His table in peace. Until then, we treasure the moments when strangers become friends, and when our home becomes a place where love builds bridges that differences cannot tear down.

5. Live a Holy and Vigilant Life

Spiritual discipline is essential for those called to watch.

- ✡ **Pursue holiness:** Whenever the Holy Spirit convicts about sin, confess and repent; learn about ungodly covenants and renounce the ones that are revealed to you and cultivate a life pleasing to God.

- ✡ **Practice fasting and worship:** These spiritual disciplines sharpen our sensitivity and give you time to develop intimacy with the Lord.

- ✡ **Guard your heart:** Stay alert to deception, complacency, and distractions that dull your spiritual senses.

✡ **Walk with courage and integrity:** The watchman must be fearless in proclaiming truth and faithful in character.

"Be alert and of sober mind. Your enemy the devil prowls around like a roaring lion looking for someone to devour."

1 Peter 5:8

6. Be a Voice of Truth and Compassion

Your witness must reflect God's heart.

✡ **Speak truth boldly:** Share God's biblical perspective on Israel's role and destiny without fear or political bias.

✡ **Demonstrate compassion:** Reject hatred, anti-Semitism, and divisiveness. Show God's mercy through your words and actions.

✡ **Live justly:** Reflect God's justice and mercy in how you treat others, becoming a bridge rather than a divider.

This chapter invites you to move from awareness into action, grounding your watchman calling in **prayer, study, unity, practical support, holiness, and compassionate truth.**

Will you rise to this call today?

CHAPTER 12

Living as a Watchman — Perseverance, Faith, and Courage

"But he who endures to the end shall be saved."

Matthew 24:13 NKJV

The call to be a watchman is more than a passing interest or a seasonal commitment—it is a lifelong journey, marked by perseverance through trials, unwavering faith in God's promises, and bold courage to stand for truth. This chapter seeks to encourage and equip you for the path ahead, reminding you that you are not alone in this sacred responsibility.

Perseverance in the Face of Trials

The life of a watchman is not without hardship. Opposition comes from both visible and unseen enemies, discouragement threatens to sap your strength, and spiritual warfare can feel relentless. Yet the Scriptures repeatedly remind us of the importance of steadfastness. Nehemiah's example is instructive: amidst threats and intimidation, he pressed on to rebuild the walls of Jerusalem (Nehemiah 6:15–16). His perseverance resulted in a completed wall and a fearful enemy, showing that faithfulness yields victory.

The New Testament echoes this call:

> *"Consider it pure joy, my brothers and sisters, whenever you face trials of many kinds, because you know that the testing of your faith produces perseverance."*

James 1:2–3

Perseverance is not merely enduring but growing stronger through the process. It refines our character and builds resilience. Art Katz often taught that suffering and perseverance are instruments in God's hands to mould believers into His image, preparing them for their role as watchmen.

Faith That Sees Beyond Circumstances

Faith is the anchor that holds the watchman steady amid storms. It is not wishful thinking but confident trust in God's sovereign plan. The watchman learns to look beyond present difficulties, fixing their eyes on eternal realities.

Hebrews encourages believers to run the race with perseverance, *"fixing our eyes on Jesus, the pioneer and perfecter of faith"* (Hebrews 12:2). This faith refuses to be shaken by dark news or opposition because it rests on the unchanging character of God.

Romans 8:28 reminds us that *"in all things God works for the good of those who love Him."* This promise sustains watchmen when the path is unclear or the night is long. Faith fuels prayer and worship, giving strength to keep watch through every season.

Courage to Stand Alone

The watchman's role is often lonely. Speaking truth may be unpopular or misunderstood by those around you. Yet courage is not the absence of fear but obedience despite fear.

Joshua received this word from the Lord:

"Have I not commanded you? Be strong and courageous. Do not be afraid; do not be discouraged, for the LORD your God will be with you wherever you go."

Joshua 1:9

Art Katz exhorted believers to be fearless in God's strength, recognising that the message they bear may be hard but is vital. The watchman must stand firm, even if it means standing alone, knowing that their labour is not in vain.

This courage is born from an intimate knowledge of God's presence and power.

Daily Renewal and Spiritual Vitality

Perseverance and courage do not come from human willpower alone. The watchman's strength is renewed daily through communion with God. Prayer, worship, fasting, and Scripture reading are not optional but essential disciplines that maintain spiritual alertness and vitality.

Regular renewal ensures the watchman can remain vigilant and effective.

A Legacy of Faithfulness

Faithful watchmen do more than survive; they leave a legacy. One person standing firm can impact generations to come, paving the way for God's Kingdom to advance. Paul's words to Timothy resonate here:

> *"I have fought the good fight, I have finished the race, I have kept the faith."*
>
> 2 Timothy 4:7

Your faithfulness today sets the stage for what the Church and Israel can build in the future. The world desperately needs watchmen who will not quit.

The Cross and Suffering—
The Heart of the Watchman's Walk

"And He said to all, 'If anyone would come after Me, let him deny himself and take up his cross daily and follow Me.'"

Luke 9:23 ESV

The Cross: The Great Equaliser

Standing watch over Israel, the nations, and the Church requires more than knowledge or zeal—it demands a heart crucified with Christ. The Cross strips away all pride, self-reliance, and illusions of control.

"For the message of the cross is foolishness to those who are perishing, but to us who are being saved it is the power of God."

1 Corinthians 1:18

Art Katz often emphasised that the Cross is not merely an event in history but a daily lifestyle. Without embracing the Cross, the watchman cannot truly see God's heart, hear His voice, or carry the burdens laid upon him.

Jesus clearly linked discipleship to carrying the Cross:

This is a costly call, countercultural in a world that values comfort and success.

Suffering as a Pathway to Intercession

The watchman's role involves entering into the sufferings of others, especially God's covenant people Israel. This is not a call to seek suffering for its own sake but to share in the fellowship of Christ's sufferings.

"For it has been granted to you on behalf of Christ not only to believe in Him, but also to suffer for Him."

Philippians 1:29

When the Church suffers alongside Israel, its prayers are fuelled with compassion and power. Suffering purifies faith, breaks down barriers, and ignites genuine love. (Colossians 1:24)

The Hidden Strength in Weakness

The Cross reveals God's strength made perfect in human weakness. The watchman's endurance and faithfulness flow not from human effort but from God's sustaining grace.

"But He said to me, 'My grace is sufficient for you, for My power is made perfect in weakness.' Therefore I will boast all the more gladly about my weaknesses, so that Christ's power may rest on me."

2 Corinthians 12:9

This paradox is central to the watchman's walk: power comes through surrender.

Practical Steps to Embrace the Cross

- ✡ Daily Self-examination: Identify areas where pride still resides — Psalm 139:23–24

- ✡ Embracing Humility and Repentance — James 4:10

- ✡ Seeking the Spirit's Help — Romans 8:26

- ✡ Spiritual Disciplines Rooted in the Cross: Prayer; fasting; and worship

A Life Marked by Resurrection Hope

Though the Cross is heavy, it leads to resurrection victory. The watchman's journey is one of death to self and life in Christ, empowered by His resurrection power.

> *"Here is a trustworthy saying: If we died with Him, we will also live with Him."*
>
> 2 Timothy 2:11

> *"I consider that our present sufferings are not worth comparing with the glory that will be revealed in us."*
>
> Romans 8:18

This hope fuels perseverance and joy amidst trials.

Scriptures for Further Study:

✡ Nehemiah 6:15–16 — *"So the wall was completed on the twenty-fifth of Elul, in fifty-two days. When all our enemies heard about this, all the surrounding nations were afraid and lost their self-confidence, because they realised that this work had been done with the help of our God."*

✡ Psalm 27:1 — *"The LORD is my light and my salvation— whom shall I fear? The LORD is the stronghold of my life—of whom shall I be afraid?"*

✡ Isaiah 40:31 — *"But those who hope in the LORD will renew their strength. They will soar on wings like eagles; they will run and not grow weary, they will walk and not be faint."*

✡ Colossians 1:24 — *"Now I rejoice in what I am suffering for you, and I fill up in my flesh what is still lacking in regard to Christ's afflictions, for the sake of His body, which is the Church."*

✡ Psalm 139:23–24 NKJV — *"Search me, O God, and know my heart; Try me, and know my anxieties; And see if there is any wicked way in me, And lead me in the way everlasting."*

✡ James 4:10 NKJV — *"Humble yourselves in the sight of the Lord, and He will lift you up."*

✡ Philippians 4:6 — *"Do not be anxious about anything, but in every situation, by prayer and petition, with thanksgiving, present your requests to God."*

✡ Galatians 6:9 — *"Let us not become weary in doing good, for at the proper time we will reap a harvest if we do not give up."*

CONCLUSION

Embracing the Watchman's Call — A Charge to the Church

"Therefore keep watch, because you do not know the day or the hour."

Matthew 25:13

As we close this journey through Israel's modern struggle and the Church's role as watchmen, the call is clear and urgent. God is raising a generation who will stand in the gap, intercede with fervency, and act with courage and faith.

✡ **A Call to Vigilance**

Eyes open to the realities around us, hearts attuned to God's voice, hands ready to build, pray, and serve.

✡ **A Call to Partnership**

Joining with Israel in humility, love, and faithfulness, rejecting fear and prejudice.

✡ **A Call to Perseverance**

Though challenges come, watchmen empowered by the Spirit and fuelled by hope will see walls rebuilt and promises fulfilled.

This book is not just to inform—it is to inspire action. The question remains:

What part will you play in this great story?

Will you stand watch, pray fervently, and proclaim truth boldly?

Art Katz's legacy reminds us: the watchman's task is vital and urgent. The world needs faithful voices now more than ever.

APPENDIX 1

Replacement Theology

A Silent Rift in the Church

Most Christians today would agree that God is faithful, that the Bible is trustworthy, and that the gospel is for all people. Yet few realise there is a theological assumption embedded in much of Church history that contradicts all three: the belief that the Church has replaced Israel in God's plan.

This belief—commonly known as *Replacement Theology* or *Supersessionism*—has quietly shaped Christian thought for nearly two millennia. It teaches that because of Israel's rejection of Jesus Christ as the Messiah, God has transferred His covenant promises to the Church, rendering Israel spiritually obsolete. The Church, it is believed, is now the "new Israel," the true people of God.

But is that what Scripture teaches?

Defining the Issue

Replacement Theology asserts that:

- ✡ The Church has replaced national Israel as God's chosen people.

- ✡ The promises made to Israel in the Old Testament are fulfilled spiritually in the Church.

- ✡ The Jewish people no longer have a distinct or ongoing role in God's redemptive plan.

This view often goes unstated, assumed rather than taught. It subtly influences how pastors preach, how believers understand prophecy, and how the Church sees its relationship to the Jewish people.

APPENDIX 2

Rediscovering God's Covenant Through Romans 11

For too long, the Church has skimmed past Romans 11, treating it like an awkward appendix to Paul's otherwise majestic theological epistle. But what if this chapter holds one of the most strategic keys to God's end-time blueprint? What if understanding this "mystery" could reframe our eschatology, humble our ecclesiology, and ignite a revival rooted in divine order?

We are standing in the tension of a global shaking and a divine reordering. In such times, God is drawing attention to the story He has never abandoned—the story of Israel. Romans 11 is not a relic of first-century Jewish-Christian tension; it is a prophetic roadmap for a united Body, Jew and Gentile, preparing the way for the return of the King.

In these pages, we will walk through Romans 11, guided not by theological curiosity but by apostolic urgency. We will explore the deep truths of divine election, partial hardening, Gentile inclusion, and Israel's future salvation. And in doing so, we'll hear Paul's heartbeat for a Church that both understands her story and knows her role in Israel's.

Let's rediscover the Olive Tree and marvel at the mercy that grafted us in.

Has God Rejected His People? (Romans 11:1-6)

"I ask then: Did God reject His people? By no means! I am an Israelite myself."

Romans 11:1a

The Question that Demands an Answer

Paul begins this pivotal chapter by confronting a dangerous assumption: that Israel's failure to recognise their Messiah meant God had abandoned them. It's a question that has echoed through the centuries and shaped much of Christian theology: *Has God rejected His people?*

His answer is emphatic: **"By no means!"** In the Greek, *mē genoito*—"Absolutely not!" This is the strongest possible repudiation in Paul's vocabulary. From the outset, Paul affirms something foundational: **God's covenant with Israel is not nullified by Israel's current unbelief.**

The Remnant According to Grace

"So too, at the present time there is a remnant chosen by grace."

Romans 11:5

Paul draws from the story of Elijah, who, in a moment of despair, thought he was the only one left who served God. But God corrected him:

"Yet I reserve seven thousand in Israel—all whose knees have not bowed down to Baal and whose mouths have not kissed him."

1 Kings 19:18

In the same way, Paul declares that in every generation—even in times of national rejection—**God preserves a faithful remnant.**

This idea is critical. The remnant is not saved by ethnicity or performance, but by **grace.** The remnant is not proof of human faithfulness, but of God's. Paul emphasises:

"And if by grace, then it cannot be based on works; if it were, grace would no longer be grace."

Romans 11:6

God's dealings with Israel, even in their unbelief, are governed by **covenantal grace**, not human merit.

Confronting the Roots
of Replacement Theology

Romans 11:1–6 dismantles the theological underpinnings of what later became **replacement theology**—the belief that the Church has replaced Israel as God's covenant people.

Paul leaves no room for this view:

- He affirms Israel's continued identity.

- He affirms God's ongoing election.

- He affirms the presence of a believing remnant.

To say that Israel is cast off is to contradict Paul's own apostolic testimony and the nature of God's grace. **The Church is not Israel's replacement—it is a co-heir, grafted into Israel's story.**

Modern Implications: The Remnant Today

Today, there is a growing remnant of **Messianic Jews—** ethnic Jews who believe in Yeshua (Jesus) as Messiah. Their existence is not accidental; it is **prophetic evidence of God's covenantal faithfulness.**

But the remnant is not just a proof text. It's a calling. These Jewish believers carry a unique priestly role in bridging the Church and Israel, embodying God's desire for **Jew-Gentile unity in Messiah.**

As Gentile believers, we are called not to ignore them, marginalise them, or "fix" them—but to honour them, co-labour with them, and provoke them (and their brethren) to the fullness of faith and destiny.

A Word to the Gentile Church

Gentile believers must wrestle with the humility embedded in this chapter. Paul will later warn:

"Do not consider yourself to be superior to those other branches. If you do, consider this: You do not support the root, but the root supports you."

Romans 11:18

The remnant theology of Romans 11 is a theological antidote to spiritual pride. It reminds us that salvation is not a Gentile phenomenon—it is the **overflow of a Jewish covenant**, extended by grace to the nations.

This isn't about ethnic superiority; it's about **covenantal order**.

The Partial Hardening (Romans 11:7–10)

"What then? What the people of Israel sought so earnestly they did not obtain. The elect among them did, but the others were hardened."

Romans 11:7

The Tragedy and the Mystery

Romans 11:7–10 takes a sobering turn. After affirming the remnant chosen by grace, Paul turns to a painful reality: the rest of Israel was *"hardened."* This is not casual language. Paul isn't simply noting unbelief—he is pointing to a divine judgment that resulted in spiritual blindness.

But what kind of hardening is this? Is it permanent? Is it punitive? Or is it redemptive?

To understand Romans 11:7–10, we must wrestle with the tension between human responsibility and divine sovereignty. Paul is not offering cold determinism, but a profound **mystery of mercy and judgment**.

What Israel Sought—and Missed

Paul begins by summarising Israel's dilemma: *"What the people of Israel sought so earnestly they did not obtain."* What were they seeking? **Righteousness.** But rather than receiving it by faith, they pursued it through the law (see Romans 9:31–32). In doing so, they stumbled over the very stone that God laid in Zion—Yeshua.

> *"Therefore thus says the Lord GOD, 'Behold, I am the one who has laid as a foundation in Zion, a stone, a tested stone, a precious cornerstone, of a sure foundation: Whoever believes will not be in haste.'"*

> Isaiah 28:16 ESV

> *"As you come to Him, the living Stone—rejected by humans but chosen by God and precious to Him—you also, like living stones, are being built into a spiritual house to be a holy priesthood, offering spiritual sacrifices acceptable to God through Jesus Christ. For in Scripture it says: 'See, I lay a stone in Zion, a chosen and precious cornerstone, and the one who trusts in Him will never be put to shame.'"*

> 1 Peter 2:4–6

Those who responded in faith—the elect—found the righteousness they sought. But those who clung to their own works were hardened. This shows us something staggering: **zeal without revelation can lead to hardening.**

The Nature of Hardening

"As it is written: 'God gave them a spirit of stupor, eyes that could not see and ears that could not hear, to this very day.'"

Romans 11:8

Paul weaves together passages from **Deuteronomy 29:4** and **Isaiah 29:10** to describe this hardening. It is not merely the result of stubbornness; it is a **divine judgment**—God *gave* them over to a "spirit of stupor."

This is deeply unsettling. But it's not without precedent. Throughout Israel's history, periods of **divine discipline** were used not to destroy, but to awaken.

This hardening is not a final rejection—it is a strategic pause.

Paul is echoing what he will soon call a "partial hardening" (Romans 11:25), and even this is part of God's larger redemptive design: **to open a door for the Gentiles.**

David's Lament

"And David says: 'May their table become a snare and a trap, a stumbling block and a retribution for them. May their eyes be darkened so they cannot see and their backs be bent forever."

Romans 11:9–10

Quoting Psalm 69, a Messianic psalm, Paul gives voice to the judgment resting on unbelieving Israel. Their blessings—their "table"—have become traps. Their rituals, feasts, and Torah, without revelation, become stumbling blocks.

This is the tragedy of religion without revelation. And yet, the lament of David isn't the last word. Even here, judgment is not the end of the story.

Jealousy and Salvation
(Romans 11:11–15)

"Again I ask: Did they stumble so as to fall beyond recovery? Not at all! Rather, because of their transgression, salvation has come to the Gentiles to make Israel envious."

Romans 11:11

The Redemptive Chain Reaction

Paul poses another rhetorical question: *Did Israel stumble so as to fall beyond recovery?* Again, his answer is emphatic: *Absolutely not!* Their failure was not final. Instead, their stumbling initiated a divine sequence of redemptive events: **Israel's rejection opened the door to Gentile salvation, which in turn is meant to provoke Israel to jealousy.**

This passage reveals one of the most stunning truths in redemptive history: **God uses Israel's temporary failure to bless the nations, and He uses the nations to awaken Israel.**

This is not a random detour; it's a master plan.

Salvation to the Nations

Paul declares that salvation has come to the Gentiles *through Israel's trespass.* This means the Gospel didn't emerge in a vacuum—it came through Jewish rejection, persecution, and scattering. As Jewish leaders opposed the message of Jesus, Paul and others turned increasingly to Gentile audiences (Acts 13:46).

Yet this was not a shift in plan—it was the plan: **to extend covenant mercy beyond the confines of Israel.**

But it wasn't the end goal.

To Provoke Them to Jealousy

The purpose of Gentile salvation isn't just global inclusion—it's restoration. Paul says Gentile believers are meant **to provoke Israel to jealousy.**

This kind of jealousy is not petty envy. It's a holy longing—a recognition that Gentiles are experiencing intimacy, blessing, and access with *Israel's own God* through *Israel's own Messiah.*

The Church is not merely a replacement community; it is meant to be a **prophetic signpost** that stirs Israel to return to her covenant identity.

Apostolic Vision: Life from the Dead

"For if their rejection brought reconciliation to the world, what will their acceptance be but life from the dead?"

Romans 11:15

Paul envisions a future moment: when Israel as a nation turns back to Messiah, it will release something cosmic— *resurrection power*, a global awakening, *"life from the dead."*

This phrase can be taken both spiritually and eschatologically:

- ✡ Spiritually: a massive global revival.

- ✡ Eschatologically: the resurrection of the dead and the return of Jesus (Matthew 23:39).

Either way, **Israel's restoration is a catalyst for world transformation.**

The Gentile Church's Role

The Gentile Church has a calling not only to enjoy salvation, but to **steward it as a means of provoking Israel to return.** This includes:

- ✡ Living in a way that displays covenant intimacy

- ✡ Rejecting arrogance and embracing gratitude

- ✡ Praying and labouring for Jewish awakening

The Church is called to be **a priestly bridge** between the nations and the Jewish people.

The Olive Tree Revelation
(Romans 11:16–24)

"If some of the branches have been broken off, and you, though a wild olive shoot, have been grafted in among the others and now share in the nourishing sap from the olive root, do not consider yourself to be superior to those other branches. If you do, consider this: You do not support the root, but the root supports you."

Romans 11:17–18

The Mystery of the Olive Tree

Paul now unveils a powerful metaphor to describe the relationship between Israel, the Gentiles, and God's covenant promises: an olive tree.

In this image:

- ✡ The **root** represents the patriarchs and the covenant promises.

- ✡ The **natural branches** are ethnic Israel.

- ✡ The **wild branches** are believing Gentiles.

Paul declares that some natural branches were broken off due to unbelief, and wild branches were grafted in. But rather than boasting, Gentiles are warned to remain humble.

This image is not about replacement—it's about **grafting and sharing.**

Sharing in the Root

Paul emphasises that Gentile believers do not replace the root—they share in its nourishment. The promises made to Abraham, Isaac, and Jacob now bless the nations through the New Covenant in Jesus.

But the **root supports the branches,** not the other way around. Gentiles owe their spiritual inheritance to a Jewish story.

To sever the Church from Israel is to **cut it off from its own root system.**

The Danger of Arrogance

"Do not consider yourself to be superior to those other branches."

Romans 11:18a

This is a rebuke to every form of anti-Semitism or replacement theology. Gentiles are commanded to walk in reverent gratitude, not spiritual superiority.

Paul anticipates the argument: *"Branches were broken off so that I could be grafted in!"* (v.19) He acknowledges this is true—but warns that **faith, not ethnicity, is the basis for inclusion.**

If God did not spare the natural branches who stopped believing, He will not spare arrogant Gentile branches either.

Grafted In by Grace

Paul affirms the kindness and severity of God. Severity to those who fell, kindness to those who stand by faith. But that faith must be accompanied by **fear and humility.**

He then declares something shocking: **if Jewish people do not continue in their unbelief, they too will be grafted back in.**

"And if they do not persist in unbelief, they will be grafted in, for God is able to graft them in again."

Romans 11:23

This is a bold declaration of **hope for Israel's restoration.**

Cultivating a Grafting Culture

What does it mean for the Church to be grafted in?

- ✡ It means sharing the identity of Abrahamic faith.

- ✡ It means honouring the Jewish people and story.

- ✡ It means being vigilant against theological arrogance.

- ✡ It means expecting and praying for the re-grafting of the natural branches.

The Church must become a place where Jewish people can see their Messiah clearly and be grafted back in to the olive tree.

Until the Fullness Comes In (Romans 11:25-27)

"I do not want you to be ignorant of this mystery, brothers and sisters, so that you may not be conceited: Israel has experienced a hardening in part until the full number of the Gentiles has come in, and in this way all Israel will be saved."

Romans 11:25–26a

The Unveiling of a Mystery

Paul introduces this section with a solemn warning for the Gentile believers not to be conceited. He then pulls back the curtain on one of the great divine mysteries in Scripture: **Israel's partial hardening is temporary and strategic.**

This "mystery" is not a puzzle to be solved but a divine plan that was once hidden and now revealed. It involves three key components:

1. A partial hardening of Israel

2. The fullness of the Gentiles coming in

3. The salvation of all Israel

Each component carries profound theological and prophetic weight.

Partial Hardening

Israel's current spiritual blindness is not total nor permanent. It is *partial* (some believe) and *provisional* (not forever). The hardening affects many but not all. Even now, there is a faithful remnant chosen by grace.

This blindness serves a purpose: it allows time for the Gentile world to receive the Gospel.

The Fullness of the Gentiles

The phrase "fullness of the Gentiles" (*plērōma tōn ethnōn*) suggests more than a number; it implies **maturity, completion, and fruitfulness.**

This could include:

- ✡ A full number of Gentiles responding to the Gospel

- ✡ A mature Gentile Church walking in righteousness and covenant alignment

- ✡ A global witness that provokes Israel to jealousy

The Church must not only evangelise, but mature into its calling as a radiant, unified Body that reflects God's character and mercy.

All Israel Will Be Saved

This phrase is among the most debated in the New Testament. Does "all Israel" mean:

- ✡ Every individual Jew?

- ✡ A national turning of the Jewish people?

- ✡ Spiritual Israel, including Gentile believers?

Given the context, Paul likely means **national, ethnic Israel.** The salvation of Israel does not negate the need for personal faith in Yeshua. Rather, it envisions a collective turning to Messiah in the end times.

This aligns with Zechariah 12:10 and Matthew 23:39, where national Israel looks upon the One they pierced and welcomes Him.

The Deliverer from Zion

"The deliverer will come from Zion; He will turn godlessness away from Jacob."

Romans 11:26b; cf. Isaiah 59:20

Paul quotes from Isaiah to affirm that the Messiah's return is connected to **the removal of Israel's ungodliness.** This is not human achievement, but divine intervention. God Himself will turn Jacob back to righteousness.

This gives the Church a future-oriented hope: **Jesus will return to a repentant Israel.**

The Prophetic Arc

Paul is describing a prophetic sequence:

1. Israel's temporary hardening

2. Gentile inclusion and maturity

3. National Israel's salvation

4. The return of the Deliverer

This arc is not just theological—it is **missional and eschatological.**

Mercy on All (Romans 11:28-32)

"As far as the gospel is concerned, they are enemies for your sake; but as far as election is concerned, they are loved on account of the patriarchs."

Romans 11:28

The Paradox of Israel

Paul now delivers a paradox that sits at the very heart of Romans 11: **Israel is both estranged and beloved.**

Regarding the Gospel, they are seen as enemies for the Gentiles' sake. That is, Israel's resistance opened the door for Gentile salvation. But in terms of election, **they are still God's beloved**—because of the patriarchs, the promises, and God's unchanging nature.

This is the tension the Church must live with: **recognising Israel's current condition without denying her eternal calling.**

Irrevocable Callings

"For God's gifts and His call are irrevocable."

Romans 11:29

This is one of the most staggering affirmations in all of Scripture. God does not withdraw His promises.

The Abrahamic covenant, the promises to Isaac and Jacob, the Davidic throne—none of these have been nullified. Israel's rejection of Messiah has not voided God's commitment to her.

This is a blow to any theology that suggests Israel has been replaced or disqualified. **If God can cancel His covenant with Israel, what assurance do Gentiles have of their own salvation?**

Mercy Through Disobedience

"Just as you who were at one time disobedient to God have now received mercy as a result of their disobedience, so they too have now become disobedient in order that they too may now receive mercy as a result of God's mercy to you."

Romans 11:30–31

Paul offers a profound insight: God is using the disobedience of both Jew and Gentile to **highlight His mercy.**

- ✡ Gentiles were once disobedient but received mercy.

- ✡ Now Israel is disobedient, but that very mercy shown to Gentiles will provoke and lead to her own mercy.

This is not a cycle of failure; it's a **cycle of redemption.**

God is orchestrating history to magnify mercy. Human disobedience becomes the canvas on which divine compassion is displayed.

A Theological Shockwave

The implication is clear: God Himself initiated a hardening for a redemptive purpose.

To many, this is uncomfortable theology. But it's vital for understanding the heart of Romans 11. God is not cruel. He is strategic. He permits blindness for a season that He might release mercy in due time.

"For God has bound everyone over to disobedience so that He may have mercy on them all."

Romans 11:32

Mercy on All

Here is the apex of Paul's theological vision: **God's ultimate desire is to show mercy.**

All have fallen short. All are in need. And all can receive mercy.

This verse brings Jew and Gentile to the same place: not superiority, but **surrender.**

It levels the playing field and exalts the grace of God.

A Church Formed by Mercy

This revelation should form the culture of the Church:

- ✡ No arrogance
- ✡ No entitlement
- ✡ No rejection of others

Instead, we become a people of intercession, humility, and gratitude. A people shaped by **mercy received and mercy extended.**

Oh, the Depth! (Romans 11:33–36)

"Oh, the depth of the riches and wisdom and knowledge of God! How unsearchable are His judgments and how inscrutable His ways!"

Romans 11:33 ESV

A Theology of Awe

After unpacking the complexities of Israel's election, Gentile inclusion, and the mystery of divine mercy, Paul does not end with explanation—he ends with **adoration.**

This doxology is a spontaneous eruption of worship, birthed from the depths of theological reflection. **The more Paul understands God's plan, the more he is undone by wonder.**

Riches, Wisdom, and Knowledge

Paul praises the *riches* of God's grace, the *wisdom* of His unfolding plan, and the *knowledge* that governs all creation.

This is the heart of true theology: not speculation, but worship. We do not study God to master Him—we study Him to marvel.

Unsearchable and Inscrutable

Paul uses two loaded terms:

- ✡ *Unsearchable judgments*—We cannot trace God's justice system fully.

- ✡ *Inscrutable ways*—We cannot map the paths of His redemptive strategy.

This does not mean God is unknowable. It means **He is infinitely beyond us**, and yet He reveals Himself to us.

Romans 11 is a clear example: God reveals just enough of the mystery to draw us into humility, gratitude, and trust.

Who Has Known the Mind of the Lord?

"Who has known the mind of the Lord? Or who has been His counsellor? Who has ever given to God, that God should repay them?"

Romans 11:34–35

These rhetorical questions, drawn from Isaiah and Job, emphasise God's sovereignty and independence. No one advises Him. No one puts Him in their debt. **He acts from pure, sovereign mercy.**

All our theology must end here: not in pride, but in reverence.

From Him, Through Him, and For Him

"For from Him and through Him and for Him are all things. To Him be the glory forever! Amen."

Romans 11:36

This closing line is one of the most powerful summaries of biblical theology:

- ✡ *From Him*—God is the **source** of all.

- ✡ *Through Him*—God is the **sustainer** of all.

- ✡ *For Him*—God is the **goal** of all.

This includes Israel. The Church. The nations. Creation. History. **Everything exists for His glory.**

Paul ends not with a strategy, but with surrender.

A Posture for the Church

As we contemplate the mystery of Romans 11, our response must mirror Paul's:

- ✡ **Awe** over God's redemptive plan.

- ✡ **Humility** about our place in it.

- ✡ **Worship** that gives Him all the glory.

Let every doctrine lead to doxology. Let every insight produce incense.

Scriptures for Further Study:

- ✡ Romans 9:31–32 — *"But the people of Israel, who pursued the law as the way of righteousness, have not attained their goal. Why not? Because they pursued it not by faith but as if it were by works. They stumbled over the stumbling stone."*

- ✡ Deuteronomy 29:4 — *"But to this day the LORD has not given you a mind that understands or eyes that see or ears that hear."*

- ✡ Isaiah 29:10 NKJV — *"For the LORD has poured out on you the spirit of deep sleep, and has closed your eyes, namely, the prophets; and He has covered your heads, namely, the seers."*

- ✡ Psalm 69:21–22 — *"They put gall in my food and gave me vinegar for my thirst. May the table set before them become a snare; may it become retribution and a trap."*

- ✡ Acts 13:46 — *"Then Paul and Barnabas answered them boldly: 'We had to speak the word of God to you first. Since you reject it and do not consider yourselves worthy of eternal life, we now turn to the Gentiles.'"*

- ✡ Zechariah 12:10 — *"And I will pour out on the house of David and the inhabitants of Jerusalem a spirit of grace and supplication. They will look on Me, the one they have pierced, and they will mourn for Him as one mourns for an only child, and grieve bitterly for Him as one grieves for a firstborn son."*

APPENDIX 3

The Remnant

The Biblical Concept of the Remnant

The concept of a "remnant" is foundational to understanding how God works in times of judgment and renewal. Throughout the prophetic books, God repeatedly promises to preserve a faithful few, a holy seed, that will survive trials and carry His covenant forward.

✡ Isaiah 10:20–22a says, *"In that day the remnant of Israel, the survivors of Jacob, will no longer rely on him who struck them down but will truly rely on the LORD, the Holy One of Israel. A remnant will return, a remnant of Jacob will return to the Mighty God. Though your people be like the sand by the sea, Israel, only a remnant will return."*

Despite great judgment and exile, a remnant is preserved, ensuring continuity of God's promises.

- ✡ Jeremiah 23:3 promises, *"I Myself will gather the remnant of My flock out of all the countries where I have driven them and will bring them back to their pasture, where they will be fruitful and increase in number."*

- ✡ Micah 2:12 declares, *"I will surely gather all of you, Jacob; I will surely bring together the remnant of Israel. I will bring them together like sheep in a pen, like a flock in its pasture; the place will throng with people."*

- ✡ In the New Testament, Romans 11:5 teaches that even now, there is a *"remnant chosen by grace"* among Israel, emphasising that God's covenant people are preserved by His mercy, not by human effort.

This faithful remnant carries the torch of God's covenant amid apostasy and upheaval, pointing to the hope of restoration.

The Remnant in Israel

God's preservation of a remnant is not merely theoretical; it has real expression in Israel today and throughout history.

The survival of Israel as a nation and faith community is evidence of God's preserving grace.

Today, many Jewish believers who have come to faith in Yeshua (Jesus) form part of this remnant, living testimonies of God's ongoing work in Israel's spiritual restoration. The remnant is characterised by their willingness to walk humbly with God, despite opposition or societal pressures.

The Remnant in the Church

The Church, too, has its remnant—believers who embody holy boldness, watchfulness, and faithfulness in a world increasingly hostile to God's truth.

- ✡ In Revelation 12:17, the remnant is described as those *"who keep God's commands and hold fast their testimony about Jesus."* This faithful few are called to stand firm against spiritual deception and persecution.

- ✡ 2 Timothy 3:12 warns, *"In fact, everyone who wants to live a godly life in Christ Jesus will be persecuted."* The remnant embraces suffering as part of faithful discipleship.

Hebrews 12:1b encourages believers to *"run with perseverance the race marked out for us"* highlighting perseverance as a mark of the remnant.

The Church's remnant is distinguished not by popularity or numbers but by unwavering commitment to holiness, prayer, and proclamation of the gospel of Jesus Christ even under pressure.

Living as Part of the Remnant

To be part of the remnant is to embrace a lifestyle marked by:

- ✡ Suffering and Repentance: The remnant willingly endures trials and continually turns back to God in humility.

- ✡ Deep Reliance on God: Faith is refined through difficulty like gold refined in fire (1 Peter 1:6–7). As

Peter wrote, *"In all this you greatly rejoice, though now for a little while you may have had to suffer grief in all kinds of trials. These have come so that the proven genuineness of your faith—of greater worth than gold, which perishes even though refined by fire—may result in praise, glory and honour when Jesus Christ is revealed."* (1 Peter 1:6) The remnant's strength comes from trusting God's power, not their own.

✡ Courage to Stand Apart: The remnant refuses to conform to worldly pressures. Paul writes, *"That is why, for Christ's sake, I delight in weaknesses, in insults, in hardships, in persecutions, in difficulties. For when I am weak, then I am strong"* (2 Corinthians 12:10), highlighting the paradox of divine strength in human weakness.

Living as part of the remnant requires a conscious choice to walk in holiness, prayer, and faithful witness, even when it is countercultural.

The faithful remnant plays a crucial role in advancing God's purposes: the prayers, witness, and faithful lives of the remnant hasten the coming Kingdom and prepare the way for God's full restoration of all things.

Endnotes

1   *Watchman:* "Watchman" language appears prominently in Isaiah 62, Ezekiel 3 & 33, and Habakkuk 2

2   Replacement Theology (also called Supersessionism) is the belief that the Church has permanently replaced Israel in God's plan. According to this view, the covenant promises originally given to Israel—such as land, blessing, and nationhood—are either fulfilled in or transferred to the Church, while Israel is left with no continuing role apart from individual Jewish believers joining the Church. The position developed in early Christian thought and was reinforced through Church Fathers such as Justin Martyr and Augustine, shaping much of traditional Christian theology. Critics argue that it dismisses the enduring biblical promises to Israel and has historically contributed to anti-Jewish attitudes.

3   *Grafted-In Partner* refers to the understanding drawn from Romans 11, where Paul describes Gentile believers as wild olive branches "grafted in" to the cultivated olive tree of Israel. This picture emphasises that Gentile followers of Jesus are not a replacement for Israel but share in the covenant blessings and responsibilities through faith in Israel's Messiah. The term highlights partnership rather than substitution, affirming the ongoing role of Israel in God's redemptive purposes and the unity of Jews and Gentiles in one family of faith.

4   Epicentre is a metaphor often used in biblical and prophetic discussions to describe Israel—and especially Jerusalem—as the central point of God's purposes and the focal ground of unfolding world events. Just as an earthquake's epicentre is the point from which tremors spread, Israel is portrayed as the place where spiritual and historical "shakings" originate, with global impact.

5   The rebirth of Israel in 1948 refers to the establishment of the modern State of Israel on 14 May 1948, after the United Nations' 1947 partition plan and the end of the British Mandate. Seen as the political restoration of Jewish sovereignty after nearly 2,000 years, it fulfilled long-held hopes for a homeland, while immediately triggering regional conflict with surrounding Arab states.

6   The Six-Day War (June 5–10, 1967) was a brief but pivotal conflict in which Israel fought against Egypt, Jordan, and Syria. In six days, Israel achieved a decisive victory, capturing the Sinai Peninsula, Gaza Strip, West Bank, East Jerusalem, and the Golan Heights. The war reshaped Middle Eastern geopolitics, heightened regional tensions, and had lasting significance for Jewish, Christian, and Muslim perspectives on Jerusalem and the land.

7   *Olive Tree*—In Romans 11, Paul uses the image of an olive tree to illustrate God's covenant people. The natural branches represent Israel, while Gentile believers are likened to wild branches grafted in. The metaphor emphasises continuity in God's plan, Israel's ongoing role, and the shared spiritual roots of Jews and Gentiles in God's promises.

8   "The radio that changed history" refers to David Ben-Gurion's broadcast on 14 May 1948, declaring the establishment of the State of Israel. The announcement, transmitted by radio from Tel Aviv, publicly proclaimed Jewish independence and was immediately heard worldwide, marking a historic turning point.

9   The name *Ben Gurion* ("son of Gurion") is not unique to modern times. A *Ben Gurion* in the first century is better known to us as **Nicodemus**, who came to Jesus by night (John 3).

10   The Fall of Jerusalem marks the event when Roman forces under Titus destroyed Jerusalem and the Second Temple, ending the First Jewish-Roman War. This led to massive loss of life, the dispersion of many Jews, and a turning point in Jewish history, profoundly shaping both Jewish and early Christian communities.

11   The Holocaust (1941–1945) was the systematic, state-sponsored genocide of six million Jews by Nazi Germany, alongside millions of others, including Roma, disabled individuals, and political dissidents. It was rooted in long-standing anti-Semitism and racial ideology, resulting in the near-destruction of European Jewry and leaving a profound impact on global history, memory, and theology.

12   Auschwitz—The largest Nazi concentration and extermination camp, located in occupied Poland, where over 1.1 million people, mostly Jews, were murdered during the Holocaust (1940–1945). It became a central symbol of Nazi atrocities and the Holocaust's industrial-scale genocide.

13   Treblinka was one of Nazi Germany's most infamous extermination camps, operating in occupied Poland from 1942 to 1943. Primarily part of Operation Reinhard, it was designed for the systematic murder of Jews in its gas chambers, resulting in the deaths of an estimated 800,000–900,000 people, most of them Polish Jews. The camp had minimal facilities for prisoners, with most victims killed shortly after arrival. A revolt by inmates in August 1943 led to its partial destruction and eventual closure.

14   "Next Year in Jerusalem": This phrase encapsulates a central theme in Jewish liturgy and identity, symbolising the aspiration for spiritual and physical return to Jerusalem. Historically, it reflects the Jewish experience of exile and the enduring hope for redemption. The phrase has evolved over centuries, influencing Jewish thought and culture. In contemporary contexts, it continues to inspire discussions on identity, faith, and the complexities of the Israeli-Palestinian conflict.

15   Romans 11: Paul teaches that God has not rejected Israel and that Gentiles are "grafted in" by faith, highlighting God's mercy, the temporary nature of Israel's unbelief, and the shared possibility of salvation for all. The chapter closes with praise for God's wisdom and sovereignty.

      Appendix 2 discusses this more fully.

16   Anti-Semitism is hostility, prejudice, or discrimination against Jews as a religious, ethnic, or racial group. Its roots span centuries, from medieval religious accusations and economic scapegoating to modern racial ideologies, culminating in systemic persecution such as pogroms and the Holocaust. Anti-Semitism has persisted in various forms, influencing social, political, and cultural attitudes toward Jews worldwide.

17   "Christ-killers": This term reflects a historic accusation used in Christian anti-Jewish rhetoric, blaming Jews collectively for the death of Jesus. Such accusations fuelled centuries of discrimination, persecution, and violence against Jewish communities, shaping much of European anti-Semitism up to and including the modern era.

18   Pogroms were violent, organised attacks against Jewish communities, particularly in Eastern Europe and Russia from the 19th to early 20th centuries. They involved looting, destruction of property, and murder, often with tacit or explicit government approval, contributing to mass displacement, fear, and the migration of Jews to other countries.

19   In biblical theology, the "remnant" refers to a faithful subset of God's people who remain loyal despite widespread disobedience or judgment. The concept appears throughout Scripture, especially in the prophets and in Romans 11, symbolising God's faithfulness, mercy, and the hope of restoration for both Israel and the faithful.

      Appendix 3 discusses this subject more fully.

20   On 7 October 2023, Hamas launched a large-scale, coordinated attack on Israel, marking one of the deadliest days in Israeli history. The assault, dubbed "Operation Al-Aqsa Flood," began with thousands of rockets fired from Gaza, followed by armed incursions into Israeli towns such as Sderot and Ofakim. Hamas fighters breached the border, killing nearly 1,200 people—including civilians, soldiers, and foreign nationals—and taking over 200 hostages. The attack was meticulously planned over several years and executed with military precision, catching Israeli forces off guard during a holiday and Shabbat. This unprecedented assault has been described as Israel's "9/11" and led to a prolonged conflict with significant casualties on both sides.

21   Major Christian Prayer Movements Supporting Israel:

      ✡   International Christian Embassy Jerusalem (ICEJ)

          Hosts the Isaiah 62 Global Prayer Gathering, a daily online prayer initiative uniting believers worldwide to intercede for Israel.

      ✡   Christians United for Israel (CUFI)

          The largest pro-Israel Christian organisation in the U.S., with over 10 million members, CUFI mobilises prayer, advocacy, and humanitarian support for Israel.

      ✡   Eagles' Wings

          Leads a global movement to support Israel, combat antisemitism, and unite a global community through prayer and aid delivery.

✡ ONE FOR ISRAEL

An Israeli ministry offering a 31-day prayer guide, podcasts, and testimonies to help individuals and groups pray for Israel. oneforisrael.org

✡ Curt Landry Ministries

Encourages Christians to pray for Israel based on biblical principles, emphasising blessings for those who support Israel. curtlandry.com

✡ Fellowship of Israel Related Ministries (FIRM)

Provides resources for Christians to support Israel through prayer, financial blessings, and sharing the truth about Israel. FIRM Israel

✡ CBN Israel

Aims to tell the true story of Israel and sustain a movement of Christians who bless and stand with the Jewish people.

These organisations and movements provide various resources and opportunities for Christians to engage in prayer and support for Israel.

22   Informed Spiritual Warfare: This concept refers to a thoughtful, biblically grounded approach to spiritual conflict, recognising that Christians face unseen powers of evil, not just visible challenges. Key components include discerning the nature of the enemy (e.g., Satan, demons, "territorial spirits"), using the "Armour of God," employing spiritual weapons like truth, prayer, faith, righteousness, and God's Word, and maintaining vigilance against deception.

23   *God's Panoply: The Armour of God & the Kiss of Heaven* (Anne Hamilton): This devotional work explores Ephesians 5–6, especially Paul's metaphor of the "Armour of God," drawing out hidden Aramaic and Hebrew insights—including that the Hebrew word for "to kiss" can also mean "to put on armour."

Hamilton frames the spiritual armour as both protective and relational, emphasising submission, spiritual warfare, identity, and the intertwining of intimacy with faith. She treats it not just as doctrinal teaching but as a devotional lens intended to lead to healing, deeper emotional engagement, and practical spiritual growth.

Also see her Facebook post 13 March 2016

24   *Needless Casualties of War* (John Paul Jackson): This book is a cautionary exploration of spiritual warfare. Jackson argues that many Christians suffer unnecessary harm—"casualties"—because they engage in intercession or spiritual conflict without fully understanding their authority, boundaries, or the spiritual realities they are contending with.

✡   The danger of presuming spiritual authority outside God's delegated jurisdiction.

✡   How mistakes in intercession—such as engaging in warfare for the wrong motives or without requisite spiritual discernment—can actually provoke harmful counter-attacks.

✡   Practical guidelines: knowing when and how to engage, exercising authority properly, being humble, discerning, avoiding reviling spiritual beings, and aligning with God's wisdom.

✡   Purpose: to help intercessors, prayer warriors, and Christian leaders avoid spiritual pitfalls, reduce unintended spiritual damage, and engage more wisely in the spiritual battles they believe exist.

25   Anne Hamilton: Facebook post – 7 January 2021

26   Anne Hamilton: Facebook post – 29 January 2020

27   Anne Hamilton: Facebook post – 6 February 2018

28   Anne Hamilton: Facebook post – 19 April 2020

29   HITinternational (Hosting for Israeli Travellers International): A volunteer-run global network founded by a native-born Israeli, which connects Israeli travellers with Christian (and other) hosts around the world. Hosts offer hospitality in homes or via services, discounts, or accommodation to Israelis travelling abroad; service providers may also offer cultural, social or tourism-related support. HIT aims to create practical expressions of blessing toward Israelis, combining travel assistance, hospitality, and cross-cultural connection. hitinternational.net

Use of Quotes

Direct quotations from Art Katz and his theological views are quoted from his lectures, writings and personal interactions and are used respectfully for educational and prophetic engagement purposes. These are done under fair use for teaching and commentary. Art Katz's materials are publicly available through the Ben Israel Fellowship and other licensed platforms.

References

- Arthur Katz; Paul Volk. *The Spirit of Truth*. Morningstar Publications, 1993. Ben Israel Fellowship

- Derek Prince. *The Destiny of Israel and the Church: Understanding the Middle East through Biblical Prophecy*. Whitaker House, 2016

- Don Finto. *God's Promise and the Future of Israel: Compelling Questions People Ask About Israel and the Middle East*. Regal Books, 2006

- Don Finto. *Your People Shall Be My People: How Israel, the Jews and the Christian Church Will Come Together in the Last Days*. Chosen Books, 2001

- Michael L. Brown. *Our Hands Are Stained with Blood: The Tragic Story of the "Church" and the Jewish People*. Destiny Image Publishers, 1992

- Marvin R. Wilson. *Our Father Abraham: Jewish Roots of the Christian Faith*. Eerdmans Publishing Co, 1989

Web Resources

- www.benisrael.org
- www.icej.org
- www.oneforisrael.org
- artkatzministries.org

HOW I MET ART KATZ

It was sometime in 1986 when I first heard a message by Art Katz on a cassette tape entitled *"A Royal Priesthood."* I was completely blown away. The message spoke about total abandonment and radical dedication to God. It was the first time I had heard a preacher speak with such boldness, bravery, and uncompromising conviction when it came to the things of God.

Fast forward to 1995—an American missionary visited our church and handed us a small booklet titled *"Apostolic Conversion."* Once again, I was deeply impacted. The message was profound and piercing, laying out what true salvation looked like through the lens of Paul's conversion. Curious, I looked at the author's name—Art Katz. The name rang a bell. Then I remembered, this was the same man whose message I had heard years ago on cassette.

A pastor friend and I decided to write him a letter, hoping he might be willing to mentor us. To our surprise, he replied! This was before the days of email and digital communication, so receiving a personal letter from someone like him was deeply humbling. In his response,

Art expressed genuine excitement about meeting us. He even said he would like to do a conference in our city—and, of course, I said a wholehearted yes.

We worked out the details, and he came. Art stayed in our home for four days—and those four days changed my theology forever. We had many deep conversations, but one statement in particular stayed with me. He said, "Your problem is that you're reading the Bible with a Gentile mindset. To understand Scripture, you must begin to think like a Jew. The Bible was written by Jews, for Jews, and must be understood in a Jewish context."

That statement blew me away. I asked him, "But how can I have a Jewish mind when I'm not a Jew?"

His response was, "That's the challenge."

From then on, we grew close. I came to see him as a spiritual father. Every time he visited Asia, he would message me to come and meet him. His input shaped me in so many ways, and much of who I am today—how I see Scripture, how I walk with God—is because of his influence in my life.

In 1986, I first heard about Art Katz through this tape. Although this is the second copy of the original—because I lost the first one—I asked Art for another copy. It looked exactly like this one.

This is the booklet I read in 1995, given to me by an American missionary who visited our church in the Philippines.

Art, my wife Josie, and me in 1996 outside our house in the Philippines. This was his first visit to our country.

Art, a friend from Ben Israel Ministry, and me in 1996 at our home in the Philippines.

Art, some Singaporean friends, and me in Singapore in 2001 during his Singapore conference.

About the Author

Alfredo Lim has served in pastoral ministry, leadership, and ministerial training for over thirty-seven years in the Philippines, New Zealand and Australia. He was the Chairman of *Bicolandia for Christ*, a regional coalition of churches in the Philippines committed to advancing the Gospel and fostering unity in the Body of Christ.

Throughout his decades of service, he had been dedicated to equipping leaders, strengthening the Church, and proclaiming biblical truth with clarity and conviction. His ministry reflects a deep passion for the Word of God, prophetic insight, and the fulfillment of God's redemptive purposes among the nations.

Author email address: team@figtreeandthenations.com

Author website: www.figtreeandthenations.com